Bible Activities and Object Lessons for Families with Children of All Ages

Running the Race

KIRK WEAVER

To Jim Weidmann, who introduced me to the priceless joy and peace that comes from providing intentional spiritual training in the home. To my family—Kelly, Madison, and McKinley—who have embraced Family Time as a core value in our life together. And, to our unborn grandchildren and great-grandchildren, may you learn, live, and teach Jesus as our personal Savior and eternal hope.

To Martha Andeen, who models God's love in how she lives life. Martha's positive spirit encourages and blesses everyone who is fortunate to call her friend. In loving memory of her son Larry who will always be remembered for his giggles, smile, and unconditional love.

—Kirk Weaver

Table of Contents

The mission of Family Time Training is to reach future generations with the Good News of Christ by training parents to teach their children Christian principles, values, and beliefs in the home.

Vision Statement

Imagine a child who responds to the needs of others and is eager to give and share.

Imagine a child who has learned to say "no" to busyness. A child who will take time to slow down and who understands the necessity of Sabbath rest.

Imagine a child who has been trained to seek truth.

Imagine a child who lives accountable to an unseen but always present God.

Imagine a child whose best friend is Jesus.

Imagine a child who is more eager to learn about the teachings of Jesus than to watch television or play sports.

Imagine a child with an eternal perspective, a child who invests more time giving and serving than accumulating and being entertained.

Imagine hundreds and thousands, a whole generation, of children growing up to live and teach the example of Christ.

In Deuteronomy 6:7 God presents his plan for passing on a godly heritage to our children. At Family Time Training our vision is to see future generations living for Christ. First, parents are to be the primary spiritual teachers in the lives of children. Second, spiritual training is to take place 24 hours a day, seven days a week. Family Time Training is just a tool, but it is a tool God can use in your family to accomplish his vision.

Foreword

"I believe most parents who are Christian want to teach their children the faith, they just don't know how. The church is important support but primary spiritual teaching must happen in the home, otherwise, it's not going to happen."

—R.C. Sproul, theologian

Family Time is the "how to" tool parents can use to teach their children the faith at home. The organization Family Time Training equips parents with fun and exciting activities designed to teach children Christian principles, values, and beliefs.

Family Time Training was formed in response to a spiritual crisis that threatens to undermine the foundation of today's families. For generations, Christian parents have abdicated to the church their God-given role as the primary spiritual leaders for their children. The church is expected to build within the lives of children a strong spiritual foundation in just one or two hours per week. God designed spiritual training to take place 24 hours a day, seven days a week, with the parents providing primary leadership and the church providing important support. For the sake of our children we must return proactive spiritual training to the home.

Family Time Training works with churches, schools, and spiritually-based groups to teach parents how to provide home-based spiritual training. Training is provided through sermons, classes, and weekend seminars. Families receive direct support through a website (www.famtime.com), activity books, and quarterly mailings.

—Kirk Weaver

Introduction

Not long ago, my wife Kelly and I were talking with Madison on her bed in her room. She was upset with the kids at school. Some were picking on an unpopular student, playing a cruel game Madi chose not to play, and it left her separated from her girlfriends. With tears flowing down her face, Madi said, "I'm trying to be like the beans in Dad's story."

Madi was referring to a Family Time lesson. The activity is built around three pots of boiling water, with the water representing adversity. We drop a carrot into the first pot, an egg into the second, and coffee beans into the third. What choices will we make in response to the adversity we face in our lives? Do we get soft like the carrot the way Peter did when he denied Christ? Does the adversity make us hard like the egg and Pharaoh's heart? Or like the coffee beans, which can represent the example of Paul, do we influence and change the environment around us? Madi was applying a lesson that we'd taught more than four months earlier.

As a parent, you've had moments like this. You know what they're worth.

Family Time activities are simple, fun object lessons intended to teach children about life in God's world. This is a book of ideas for structured teaching times that will carry forward and open doors for informal learning moments. At first it may feel a little clumsy to create the structured time, to boil carrots and eggs and coffee beans. But the moments when your child actively chooses the godly path will fuel your love and your relationship like nothing else in the world.

"Here's the game," I told the four children, my son, daughter, and two neighborhood friends. They were standing at the bottom of the stairs, wide-eyed and eager for the Family Time activity. Standing at the top of the stairs, I said, "I represent Jesus in heaven. More than anything I want you up here with me, but, you can't use the stairs and you can't use the handrails."

They knew there was a trick, something to learn. But what? How would they get from the bottom of the stairs to the top without touching the stairs or the railing? My daughter ran to get a laundry basket, turned it upside down, stood on top and reached up only to find she was still more than fifteen steps from the top.

It was my son, Mac, the youngest of the four, who figured out the solution. "I got it! Dad, please come down and get me," his face beaming, because he had solved the riddle. I descended the stairs.

"Will you carry me to the top?" he asked. "Of course!" I responded. After carrying all four children piggyback style to the second floor, I said, "That's how you get to heaven. You can't do it on your own. Only through Jesus can you get there." A powerful lesson presented in the language of children that they still remember to this day.

Deuteronomy 6:5-9 says:

> *"Love the LORD your God with all your heart and with all your soul and with all your strength. These commandments that I give you today are to be upon your hearts. Impress them on your children."*

How?

> *"Talk about them when you sit at home and when you walk along the road, when you lie down and when you get up. Tie them as symbols on your hands and bind them on your foreheads. Write them on the doorframes of your houses and on your gates."*

How will we shape our children? What mark will we leave upon them? Is it possible that we can launch them into the world stronger, purer, more trusting of God than we were? Is it possible that we can reshape our families and our family interactions around the joy of loving God with all that is within us?

I believe it is possible. That's what this book is for.

The ABC's of Effective Family Times

A Attention Span: The rule of thumb for attention span is one minute for each year of age. A three-year-old may have a three-minute attention span. Break up your Family Time into three-minute increments. With variety, you gain additional attention span. For example:

3 minutes	Sing or play your Family Time theme song
2 minutes	Pray
3 minutes	Tell the story
3 minutes	Demonstrate the object lesson
3 minutes	Let the child repeat the object lesson
3 minutes	Retell the story
2 minutes	Practice memorization
2 minutes	Close in prayer
21 minutes	Total Family Time

B Be Prepared to Say "I Don't Know": Your children WILL ask you a question that you cannot answer. Promise to find the answer and get back to them within 24 hours. You can call a pastor or search the Internet for more information.

C Call it Family Time: When your children grow up you want them to have fond, lasting memories of Family Time. When referring to your times of formal spiritual training, say "Family Time" often. In the same way your children will remember going to school and church or playing sports and music, they will remember times of spiritual training called "Family Time."

D Drama Queens and Kings: Kids love to put on plays. Pick a Bible Story, assign the roles from Director to Diva—everyone gets in on the act. Don't forget to assign a videographer so you can watch it later.

Encourage Guessing: Answering a question involves risk. Your child's answer may be right or wrong. Praise him when he guesses at an answer. If he gives the wrong answer say, "Great guess! The answer is..." and give him the correct information. This will keep him participating. If you say, "No, that's wrong," children may eventually stop talking.

Fixed or Flexible: It's great and admirable to have Family Time the same night every week. However, it may not be practical for your family. Be willing to move the night if needed. The important thing is to have at least one Family Time each week.

Give it to God: God commands parents and grandparents to be spiritual teachers with their children (Deuteronomy 6:7; Deuteronomy 4:9, Psalm 78:5). Trust that God will equip you to fulfill his plan. As you prepare, and before you begin your Family Time each week, pray and ask the Holy Spirit to lead you and clearly communicate the message to your children.

Hold the Distractions: When sitting at the table, remove the centerpiece, pencils, paper...anything that can distract a child. A random paper clip left on a table can lead to a possession battle that will ruin the atmosphere for Family Time. Also, when using materials like balloons, string, etc., don't bring them out until you're ready to use them.

Involve Kids in the Preparations: Whenever possible, especially as kids get a little older, involve kids in the lesson preparations. Preparation can be as much fun as doing the activity and certainly increases ownership. Kids will enjoy making an obstacle course, building a tent with sheets, or mixing a big batch of cornstarch.

Just Do It!: Don't wait another day to get started!

Kitchen Table: Start your Family Time at the kitchen table even if you are only going to be there for a few minutes. Chairs provide natural boundaries that will help children focus as you explain what will happen during the Family Time.

L **Listen to the Holy Spirit:** Be prepared to modify or change the discussion if the Spirit moves the conversation in a different direction.

M **Make a Picture:** Coloring a picture to reinforce a Bible Story can be an excellent teaching technique. While the family is coloring, great conversation about the lesson can take place.

N **Not a Spectator Sport:** Participate with your children in the game or activity. By participating, you show your kids that you value Family Time.

O **Oh Boy!** If you're feeling frustrated or if family members have a negative attitude—reschedule. Keep it positive.

P **Play it Again, Sam:** For younger children, put the lesson into a one sentence phrase like: "Noah had faith in God." Or, "Be content with what God sent." The same night at bedtime, remind children of the main point. The following morning ask them what they remember from Family Time the night before.

Q **Quitting isn't an Option:** Commit to once a week and do your best not to take a week off. Continue to do Family Time during the summer months. If you stop, your kids will sense a lack of commitment to Family Time on your part.

R **Repetition isn't the Same as Redundant:** Younger children learn best through repetition. In the same way they will watch a video over and over, they may want to repeat fun Family Time activities. Be prepared to repeat the activity, asking the children to explain what the different elements represent. Consider repeating with neighborhood children; your children will learn even more when they teach others.

S **Simple Structure:** Younger children benefit from a structured time together. Consider following the Family Time Format each week.

T **To Be or Not to Be Silly:** Model for your children that it's okay to be dramatic, silly, and have fun. Kids love it when their parents are playful.

U **Unique Locations:** Have a church service in a crawl space to represent the early church under persecution. Hold your Family Time outside at a neighborhood park. Repeat fun activities when visiting relatives on vacation. Tell the story of Zacchaeus while sitting in a tree house. Changing the setting of your Family Time can be fun.

V **Variety:** Using a video clip can be an excellent way to teach a lesson. However, using video clips three weeks in a row becomes predictable and is less effective. Mix up the format and tools you use in your weekly Family Time (coloring, video clips, a snack tied to the lesson, etc.).

W **Watch Out for Unrealistic Expectations:** Family Time is seldom a disappointment to children. However, parents may sometimes feel like the lesson did not go as well as they had hoped. Often this disappointment is directly related to the parent's expectations. Keep in mind that kids learn valuable things over time. You don't have to get something fantastic out of each Family Time. Be prepared to learn right along with your kids.

X **Xpect a Future:** One day your children will grow up and start families of their own. As your children raise your grandchildren they will be equipped with positive memories and effective tools to pass along the faith of their fathers.

Y **Y? Y? Y?** Questions are cool. Frederick Beuchner says, "If you want big answers then ask small questions." "What did you learn at Sunday School?" is a big question. "Who did you sit next to at Sunday School?" is a smaller question that can lead to more discussion.

Z **Zees ees Fun!** Remember the most important things you can do: take your time, engage your child, and have fun together. A silly accent never hurts either!

Family Time Format

The "Family Time Format" is a simple structure that families can use when leading a Family Time activity. You may want to tweak and modify the structure to meet the needs of your family.

Younger children benefit from using the same format from week to week. They may want to repeat the activity again and again. Remember, repetition is how young children learn. Be sure to call your time together "Family Time." When your kids are grown, you want them to look back and be able to identify times of formal spiritual training in the same way they can identify school, sports, and church.

Families of older children may want to make the lesson less formal. For example, you may not have a "Family Time Theme Song." Instead, you can invite your teens to share a favorite song. Ask them why they like the song. Is it the beat, the singer, the words?

Meet Weekly:

The goal is to lead a weekly Family Time in your home. Try to designate and reserve the same time each week, recognizing that on occasion you will need the flexibility to schedule around conflicts.

No Fuss Dinner:

Plan a simple dinner so that everyone in the family can participate. You don't want one parent spending a lot of time fixing the meal and another parent spending a lot of time cleaning up. Minimize dinner preparation and clean-up by using paper plates and paper cups. Just by looking at how the table is set, children will know it's Family Time night. You may want to use leftovers or order in dinner. Keep it simple.

Discuss the Previous Family Time:

During dinner talk about what the family did last week during Family Time. Challenge the children to try and remember the activity and message. Talk about the highlights and use this time to reinforce the message and its potential application during the past week.

You'll be surprised to learn that children will remember back two weeks, three weeks, maybe more.

Family Time Theme Song:

Pick your own family "theme song." Since this is for your spiritual training time, consider songs that talk about faith, family, relationships, and love.

Play this song after dinner and just before the evening lesson and activity. Younger children like to create a dance or hand motions to go with the song. This song signals that Family Time is here while building excitement and anticipation.

SONG IDEAS:
"The Family Prayer Song (As For Me and My House)" by Maranatha
"Creed" by Rich Mullins

Prayer:

Open the Family Time with prayer. Children and parents can take turns. Teach the children to pray about a wide variety of topics, joys, and concerns.

Message:

Decide in advance and practice the activity you will use. Communicate clearly the main principle or value being taught through the lesson.

Object Lesson:

Each Family Time has an object lesson or activity that reinforces and helps children remember the main message.

Memorize:

Repeat the short, rhyming phrase included with the lesson. The rhyme is designed to help children remember the lesson.

Prayer:

Close the time together with a prayer. Tie the prayer to the lesson. Try different methods of prayer such as holding hands and praying, pray from oldest to youngest, or say "popcorn" prayers (one- or two-word prayers about a specific topic).

Plan Ahead for Next Week:

Many lessons require that you gather specific objects or purchase items from the store. Look ahead to next week's Family Time activity to make sure you have all the necessary ingredients.

Lesson 1:
GOD'S WORD—THE SWORD FOR BATTLE

TEACHING GOAL: Follow God's Word when you are tempted to make bad choices.

1. Play theme song
2. Pray
3. Lesson and discussion
4. Memorize: **God's Word we obey; to chase Satan away.**
5. Close in prayer

SCRIPTURE: Ephesians 6:10-18 When the bad day comes, you can stand your ground by putting on the armor of God that includes the sword of the Spirit, the Word of God.

Matthew 4:1-11 The Temptation of Jesus

MATERIALS: Pie pan and water
Pepper
Paper and pen
Eyedropper
Soap or liquid detergent

Words that are written in **bold** are when you, the parent, are speaking. Feel free to use your own words.

Big Idea

Paul, one of the first Christians, wrote a book to the church in a town called Ephesus. He told the people that if they wanted to fight Satan and keep from making bad choices, then they needed to put on the armor of God, including the sword of God's Word. God gives us his Word in the Bible.

There was a time when Jesus was tempted to make bad choices, and he used God's Word (the sword) to fight Satan. Jesus went into a desert. He did not eat for 40 days. Satan came to him and tried to get Jesus to make bad choices. Three times Satan told Jesus to make bad choices, and three times Jesus quoted what God says in the Bible. Jesus refused to make the bad choices Satan wanted him to make, and after the third time, Jesus told Satan to flee and he did.

We can use what God says just like Jesus did to make good choices and cause Satan to flee from us.

EXAMPLES:

- When we are tempted to make a bad choice by saying something bad, we can remember that God says to encourage one another and build each other up.

- When we are tempted to make a bad choice by saying, "No. I don't want to go to bed," we can remember that God says to obey your parents.

- When we are tempted to make a bad choice by saying something that is not true, we can remember that God says to tell the truth.

- When we are tempted to make a bad choice by taking something that does not belong to us, we can remember that God says not to steal.

Activity

Take a pie pan and fill just the bottom with water. The pan symbolizes the desert. Put the stick figure on a small piece of paper in the middle of the pan to represent Jesus. Shake pepper into the pan, and it will float on top of the water. The pepper symbolizes bad choices and Satan surrounding Jesus in the desert. Put liquid soap into an eyedropper. The soap and dropper symbolize the Word of God. Squeeze only one drop of soap near the figure of Jesus, and the pepper will flee to the side of the pan. This symbolizes Jesus using God's Word to cause Satan and bad choices to flee.

Repeat the activity again, but the second time allow the children to tell what each thing represents. Be sure to completely clean all the soap out of the pan before you try it again or the activity won't work.

Application

Every person experiences temptation. Here are some examples of temptations to discuss with your kids.

- I feel like hitting my brother.
- I thought about lying so that no one knew that I broke it.
- I was going to just push the junk under my bed instead of cleaning it up nicely.
- I wanted to be mean to my friend because she was ignoring me.

One of the ways God wants us to deal with temptation is to know the Scriptures and use them to fight off those temptations in our lives. The Bible is an amazing book and it helps us be strong on the inside instead of weak. Then we don't have to fall to temptation. We can trust God and use his Sword to fight it off. Let's work on dealing with temptation in our lives this week.

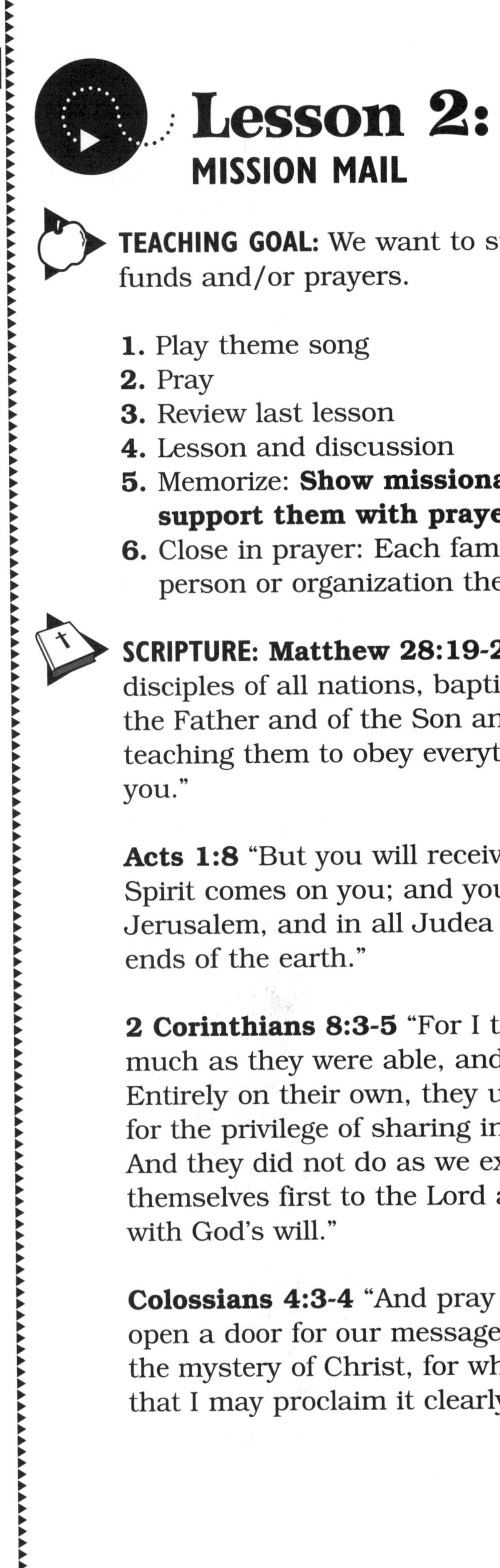

Lesson 2:
MISSION MAIL

TEACHING GOAL: We want to support missionaries with funds and/or prayers.

1. Play theme song
2. Pray
3. Review last lesson
4. Lesson and discussion
5. Memorize: **Show missionaries you care; support them with prayer.**
6. Close in prayer: Each family member pray for the person or organization they chose.

SCRIPTURE: Matthew 28:19-20 "Therefore go and make disciples of all nations, baptizing them in the name of the Father and of the Son and of the Holy Spirit, and teaching them to obey everything I have commanded you."

Acts 1:8 "But you will receive power when the Holy Spirit comes on you; and you will be my witnesses in Jerusalem, and in all Judea and Samaria, and to the ends of the earth."

2 Corinthians 8:3-5 "For I testify that they gave as much as they were able, and even beyond their ability. Entirely on their own, they urgently pleaded with us for the privilege of sharing in this service to the saints. And they did not do as we expected, but they gave themselves first to the Lord and then to us in keeping with God's will."

Colossians 4:3-4 "And pray for us, too, that God may open a door for our message, so that we may proclaim the mystery of Christ, for which I am in chains. Pray that I may proclaim it clearly, as I should."

MATERIALS: In advance collect mail from missionaries, missions, and nonprofits for one month
Map of the world, country, state, and/or city
Stickers or markers to use on the maps

Words that are written in **bold** are when you, the parent, are speaking. Feel free to use your own words.

Big Idea

In his last words, Jesus directed his followers to go throughout the world spreading the Good News and teaching people about Jesus. Do you know what "Good News" means? Listen to answers. The Good News is that God sent his son, Jesus, so that whoever believes in him can spend eternity with God in heaven. Ask for volunteers to read Matthew 28:19-20 and Acts 1:8.

The Apostle Paul was one of the early Christians who went out into the world to tell others about Jesus. Paul was a Jew sent by Jesus to tell the Gentiles the Good News. Today we use the name "missionary" to describe Christians like Paul who go to Africa, China, other parts of America, and other parts of our state and city to tell people about Jesus.

Activity

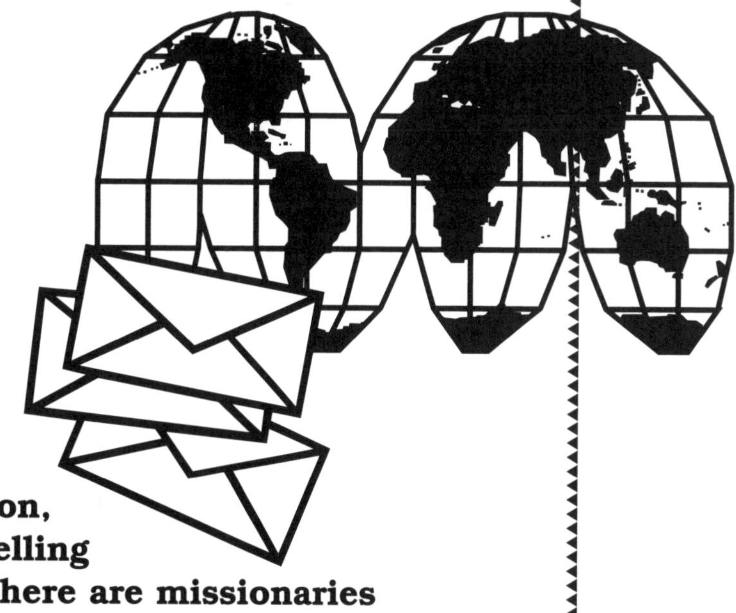

Ask for volunteers to read 2 Corinthians 8:3-5 and Colossians 4:3-4. **Just like Paul, missionaries today need the financial support and prayers of Christians. When writing to the Colossians, Paul was in prison, in chains, because he was telling others about Jesus. Today there are missionaries in prison for telling others about Jesus.**

We are each going to choose a missionary to {support financially or pray for or both}. I've been saving our mail for the past month. We are going to divide the mail into three piles.

PILE #1: **Missionaries, missions, and organizations we already support.** Explain why you support these causes.

PILE #2: **Missionaries, missions, and organizations we choose not to support.**

PILE #3: **Missionaries, missions, and organizations we don't currently support but would consider supporting.** Explain why. As you talk about each cause in piles #1 and #3, mark their location on the maps.

Application

Encourage each family member to choose someone new to support. Have each person explain why they chose their particular person or organization. Set up a plan and reminder so that the family prays (and/or makes gifts) on a regular basis.

Lesson 3:
MIRROR

By N.K. Thomas (India)

TEACHING GOAL: The Bible is a mirror that will show what is right and what is wrong.

1. Play theme song
2. Pray
3. Review last lesson
4. Lesson and discussion
5. Memorize: **In the mirror I can see; it's like the Bible that guides me.**
6. Close in prayer

SCRIPTURE: James 1:22-25 "Do not merely listen to the word, and so deceive yourselves. Do what it says. Anyone who listens to the word but does not do what it says is like a man who looks at his face in a mirror and, after looking at himself, goes away and immediately forgets what he looks like. But the man who looks intently into the perfect law that gives freedom, and continues to do this, not forgetting what he has heard, but doing it—he will be blessed in what he does."

MATERIALS: Mirror
Masking tape and pen
Q-tips or cotton swabs
Washable paint
Water
Light corn syrup
2 small cups

Words that are written in **bold** are when you, the parent, are speaking. Feel free to use your own words.

Big Idea

Ask someone to read James 1:22-25. **This verse says do not just listen to the Bible, do what it says. Those who listen**

to the Bible but don't do what it says are like people who look in a mirror and walk away without doing anything about what they see. Why do we look into a mirror? Listen to answers. To see how I look. Is my hair a mess? Do I have food on my face? Acne? **It would be silly to look in a mirror, see jelly and dirt all over, acne ready to pop and hair sticking out everywhere, then just walk out the door and go to school without doing anything. Why even look in the mirror if you're not going to change what is wrong?**

The verse also tells us that the man who looks into the perfect law, which is the Bible—God's perfect directions for living—and does what it says, will be blessed. This is like the person who looks in the mirror, cleans her face, combs her hair, and will go outside looking clean and ready.

B Activity

Let's think of some ways this will work using the Ten Commandments (Deuteronomy 5). **For example, let's say I tell a lie, commandment #9. Afterward I read the Bible and I'm reminded that God tells me not to lie. If I hear the words and do nothing about it, I am like the man who looks in the mirror and walks away! If I hear the words and then apologize for the lie and ask God to help me not lie in the future, I am like the person who looks at the Bible and does what it says. My life will be blessed if I keep looking at the Bible and doing what it says.**

Let others take turns following your example and explaining how this verse works with:

- **COMMANDMENT #10 DO NOT COVET.** Wanting a toy/game someone else has. Wanting it so badly that you have a bad attitude, whine, and complain about not having it.

- **COMMANDMENT #8 DO NOT STEAL.** Borrowing a toy or game. Knowing it's time to give it back but you keep it, hoping your friend won't remember you still have it.

- **COMMANDMENT #5 HONOR YOUR FATHER AND MOTHER.** Your parents ask you to do a chore and you say "No" in an angry voice and refuse to obey or just act like you didn't hear them.

- **COMMANDMENT #3 USING THE NAME OF GOD OR JESUS AS A CURSE.** You get mad and curse at others.

Write the word "Bible" on the masking tape and put it on the top of the mirror. In a small cup, mix up the paint so that it is a bright color AND a watery consistency. In another small cup mix 2 tablespoons of water with a teaspoon of light corn syrup. Dip one end of the Q-tip cotton swab into the paint and the other end into the water/syrup mixture. Choose one child to go first. Have the child close her eyes and then touch her on the forehead, both cheeks, chin, and ears. Touch her face with the water/syrup end of the Q-tip except for one time when you touch her face with the paint end of the Q-tip.

Have the child guess which spot on her face is paint. After guessing, have her look into the mirror and see if she is correct. **The mirror shows us where the paint is so that we can wipe it clean. In the same way, the Bible shows us the sin/wrong in our life so we can clean it up.**

Repeat the activity with each family member.

Application

Growth happens in our lives when we're willing to admit areas of weakness and work on making them strong. The Bible gives a continual mirror to help us grow and develop.

Lesson 4:
JOSIAH

TEACHING GOAL: We need to know God's Word, the Bible, in order to understand how God wants us to live.

1. Play theme song
2. Pray
3. Review last lesson
4. Lesson and discussion
5. Memorize: **We are pleasing in God's sight; when we do what he says is right.**
6. Close in prayer

SCRIPTURE: 2 Kings 22 to 2 Kings 23:30 Josiah

MATERIALS: Puzzle design
Cardboard
Paper and pen
Blindfold
Stapler or tape
A treat for the children

IN ADVANCE: Using the pattern at the end of this lesson, trace the five pieces of the game onto cardboard or heavy paper. Cut out the pieces so that they can be used as a puzzle in the activity. Draw a diagram of how the pieces should fit together into a square. Put the diagram in a little book you have created using pieces of paper and a stapler or tape. Hide the book in the clothes dryer.

Words that are written in **bold** are when you, the parent, are speaking. Feel free to use your own words.

Big Idea

Josiah was eight years old when he became King of Judah. Who do we know who is eight years old? What would it be like to be an eight-year-old king? Josiah's

father set a bad example for Josiah. His father Amon was a King who "did evil in the eyes of the Lord." Josiah's dad worshiped idols and did not follow the commandments of the Lord.

But Josiah chose to be a good king. "He did what was right in the eyes of the Lord." He followed the ways of the Lord like the good King David before him.

When he was 26 years old, Josiah hired people to repair the temple (the temple was their church). The priest at the temple (the priest is like our pastor) found the Book of the Law (God's instructions) that had been lost.

After King Josiah read the Book of the Law, he was very sad because he realized that his people were not doing what God wanted them to do. So he tore his clothes. When people tore their clothes in that time it meant that they were very sad.

Josiah asked the priest to pray to the Lord and ask God about what was written in the Book of the Law. The priest prayed. The Lord was angry because the kings of Judah had not obeyed the words in the Book of the Law.

Josiah learned that God was planning to bring disaster on his country, Judah, because the people were not following the Lord's commandments. They were doing things like worshiping idols.

When Josiah heard about the coming disaster, he humbled himself before God and turned his heart toward God. And because he was so sad and cried when he learned that they had not been following God, the Lord delayed the disaster so that Josiah could live his life in peace.

So Josiah read the Book of the Law out loud to the people. Josiah renewed his commitment to the commandments in the Book of the Law. He pledged to follow the commands, regulations, and decrees with

all his heart and soul. The people then also pledged to follow the Book of the Law.

Josiah had all the idols destroyed from all over the country of Judah. Josiah told people to start celebrating the Passover again. It had been hundreds of years since the people had celebrated the Passover as it was written in the Book. Josiah was king for 31 years before he was killed in a war against the Pharaoh named Neco in Egypt.

"Neither before nor after Josiah was there a king like him who turned to the LORD as he did—with all his heart and with all his soul and with all his strength, in accordance with all the Law of Moses." (2 Kings 23:25)

B Activity

(Similar to pin the tail on the donkey.) One adult plays the role of "Lord." Another adult is the spinner. Each child takes a turn being blindfolded in the center of the open area and playing the part of "Josiah." After the child is blindfolded, the adult who plays the "Lord" picks a place to stand until the child's turn is completed. The spinner-adult spins the child until the child is not sure of his or her place in the room. The child can then choose to: 1) Point in the direction where they guess the "Lord" is standing, or 2) Ask for help to which the "Lord" will respond with up to three short whistles, after which the child must point.

Take the blindfold off and see how close the child was to pointing at the "Lord."

This game represents Josiah turning to the Lord. The Bible says that no other king turned their heart to the Lord like Josiah did. The three whistles represent the help that the Book of the Law provided in finding what the Lord wanted Josiah to do.

If a child doesn't ask for help and points in the wrong direction, this represents what life was like for Josiah before he found the Book of the Law. If the child asks for help and still does not point at the "Lord" after the three whistles, point out how the whistles (Book of the Law) got him closer to the "Lord."

IMPORTANT LESSONS FROM THE STORY OF JOSIAH

- **Josiah's father set a bad example by doing things that were wrong. But Josiah chose to follow God's way instead of his father's bad example.**

  What do we do when someone sets a bad example for us? Do we follow God's way or our own way?

  EXAMPLES:
  1. A friend comes over to play and wants us to break one of the rules in our house.
  2. We go over to a friend's house and they are watching a movie that has bad words or fighting that we know Mom and Dad wouldn't want us to watch.
  3. We break one of the rules and think that if we lie, then we won't get in trouble.

- **When Josiah read the Book of the Law and learned what was right, he changed his ways and stopped doing what was wrong. Instead he started doing what God wanted.**

  Sometimes we don't even realize that things we are doing are wrong. Sometimes we hear words or jokes at school and when we repeat them at home, Mom or Dad say, "That's a bad word or a cruel joke, and it may hurt someone's feelings." When we learn that something is hurtful, we need to stop repeating the word or joke and do what is right.

- **When Josiah heard that God was planning to destroy the people, he didn't get mad. Instead he was very sad and he cried. He was not proud. Instead he was humble.**

When we find out that we have been doing something wrong, do we try to defend our actions to make them seem not so bad? Do we argue that what we did wasn't wrong? Josiah's example teaches us to be humble and sad and most importantly, to change our ways.

- **God saw the true repentance that was in Josiah's heart and changed his punishment, delaying the disaster until after Josiah died.**

  God sees what is in our hearts, and when we change our ways and repent, he may respond differently than if we continue making bad choices.

Mix up the pieces of the cardboard puzzle and instruct the kids to use all five pieces to make a perfect square. Give the kids three minutes to finish the task. Tell them that if they finish in time, then they will receive a treat.

NOTE: The kids are not supposed to be able to accomplish the task in the time provided (you may need to shorten the time for older children).

When time runs out, sigh and say, **Oh, that's too bad, looks like we don't get the treat.** Before the kids can complain, immediately say in a louder voice filled with excitement, **Wait a minute! I remember there is a book with instructions on how to put the puzzle together! I lost it, but maybe you can find it. The only clue I have is that I remember it was in the pocket of my jeans before they went into the dryer, and it wasn't in my jeans when they came out of the dryer.**

When the kids find the book with the directions, allow them to complete the puzzle. This time they should be able to put the puzzle together easily.

Application

Tell the kids, **This is just like the story of Josiah. Josiah and the people of Judah were living their lives the wrong way, like we were putting the puzzle together the wrong way. Then Josiah found the Book of the Law that told the people how to live a life pleasing to God, like we found a book that told us how to put together the puzzle. In the same way that God changed his plan to bring disaster on Josiah and instead gave him peace, I'm going to change my plan of not giving you a treat and instead I'm going to give you a treat.**

We need to read and do what it says in God's Word, the Bible. It pleases God and keeps us from doing the wrong things.

JOSIAH PUZZLE

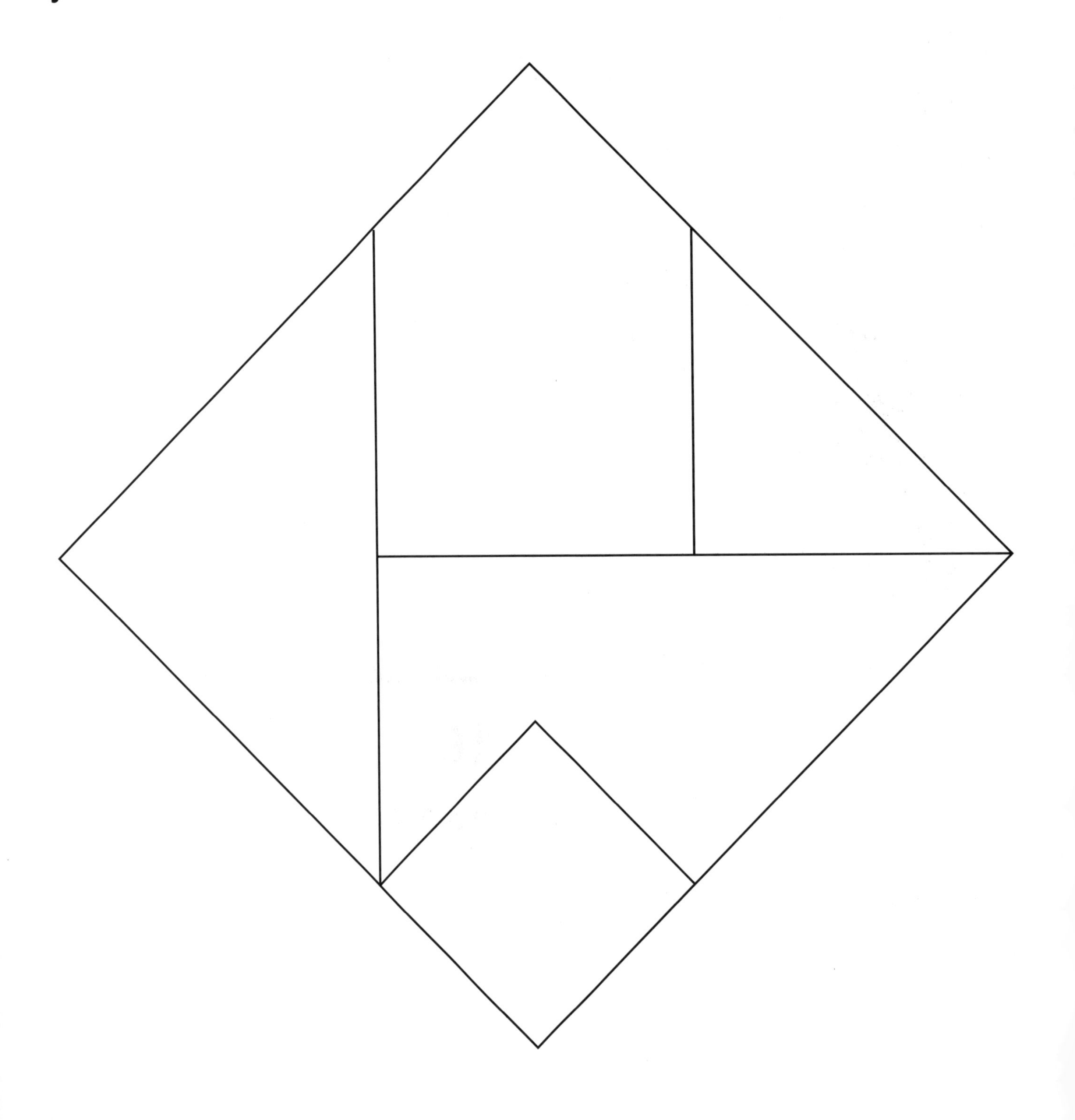

Lesson 5:
JESHUA

TEACHING GOAL: God protects us from Satan and evil.

1. Play theme song
2. Pray
3. Review last lesson
4. Lesson and discussion
5. Memorize: **I am not a loser; Jesus says, "Enough!" to Satan the accuser.**
6. Close in prayer

SCRIPTURE: Zechariah 3:1-2 "Then he showed me Joshua [Jeshua] the high priest standing before the angel of the LORD, and Satan standing at his right side to accuse him. The LORD said to Satan, 'The LORD rebuke you, Satan! The LORD, who has chosen Jerusalem, rebuke you! Is not this man a burning stick snatched from the fire?'"

Zechariah 10:4 "From Judah will come the cornerstone, from him the tent peg."

Luke 22:31-32 "Simon, Simon, Satan has asked to sift you as wheat. But I have prayed for you, Simon, that your faith may not fail. And when you have turned back, strengthen your brothers."

MATERIALS: Campfire
Long stick

Words that are written in **bold** are when you, the parent, are speaking. Feel free to use your own words.

Big Idea

God protects us. When parents and children get a glimpse of this reality, they become extremely grateful for the Lord's work. Use this lesson to point out the protection of God on your family.

B Activity

Make sure the long stick is in the campfire and is charred or burning. While building and sitting around the campfire, give the background and tell the story of Jeshua.

We are going to learn the story of Jeshua. Does anyone know about Jeshua? Listen to answers. **The story of Jeshua is found in the Old Testament in the book of Zechariah. Jeshua lived in a dangerous and exciting time. The Israelites, God's chosen people, had been taken captive by the enemy, the Babylonians. Many Israelites had been killed and their cities, including Jerusalem, had been destroyed. For years, the surviving Israelites lived as captives spread across the foreign lands of Babylon. Finally, it was time for the Israelites to go home. God was calling his people out of captivity in foreign lands to return to their home in Jerusalem.**

Jeshua was the high priest, like an important pastor or church leader today, during this exciting time. God called Jeshua to be a leader of the Israelites as they returned to Jerusalem.

Does anyone know who Zechariah is? Listen to answers. **Zechariah was a prophet who lived at the same time as Jeshua. God would give messages to Zechariah in visions, and Zechariah had a vision about Jeshua.**

The vision: Jeshua was standing between an angel and Satan. Satan was accusing Jeshua of many things. But in the vision, God says to Satan, "Enough!" God rebukes Satan and stands up for Jeshua. God compares Jeshua to a burning stick that is snatched from the fire. Read Zechariah 3:1-2.

Pull the long stick out of the fire. It should be charred or burning. USE CAUTION AND BE SAFE! **What do you think God was saying when he compared Jeshua to a burning stick snatched from the fire?** Listen and encourage guesses. **Who is the stick? What is the fire? What is the charred part of the stick? Who pulls the stick out of the fire?** The charred wood might represent the things Satan accused Jeshua of doing. If God had not protected Jeshua, he might have been destroyed by the bad things just like this fire would destroy the stick.

Application

How does this story apply to our lives? How could your life or someone else's life be "charred" today? How does Satan try to accuse you of mistakes you've made or problems you struggle with? Can you sense God standing up for you saying, "Enough. Get away, Satan." God wants to forgive our sins, while Satan just wants to torment us with guilt over our sins.

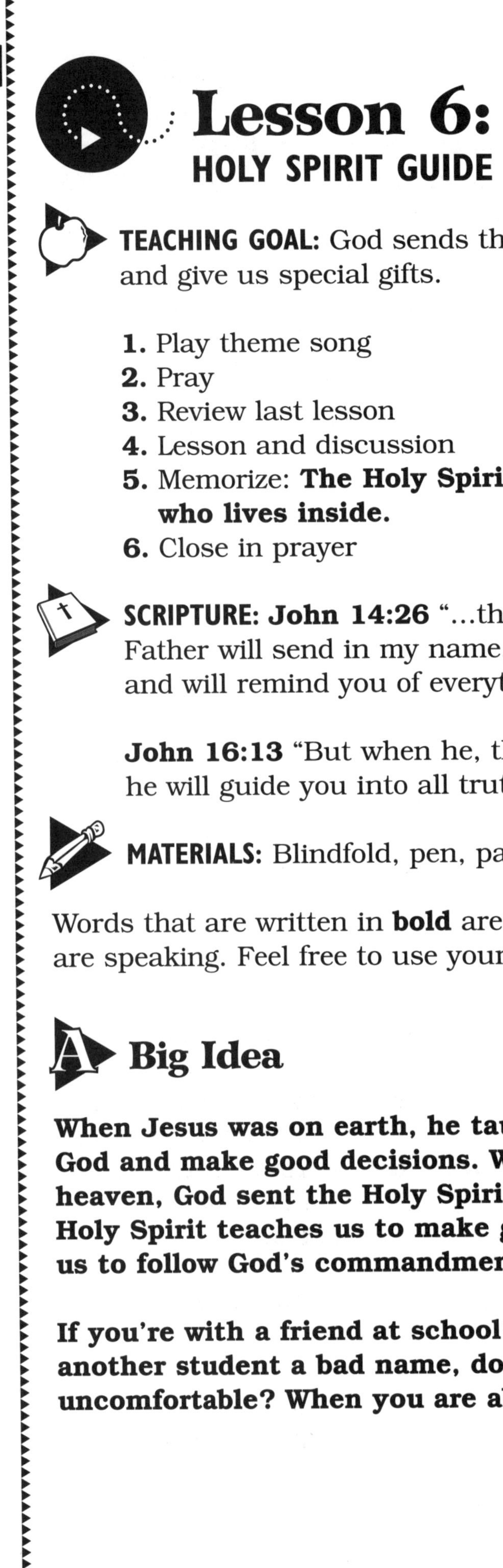

Lesson 6:
HOLY SPIRIT GUIDE

TEACHING GOAL: God sends the Holy Spirit to guide us and give us special gifts.

1. Play theme song
2. Pray
3. Review last lesson
4. Lesson and discussion
5. Memorize: **The Holy Spirit: our guide who lives inside.**
6. Close in prayer

SCRIPTURE: John 14:26 "...the Holy Spirit, whom the Father will send in my name, will teach you all things and will remind you of everything I have said to you."

John 16:13 "But when he, the Spirit of truth, comes, he will guide you into all truth."

MATERIALS: Blindfold, pen, paper

Words that are written in **bold** are when you, the parent, are speaking. Feel free to use your own words.

Big Idea

When Jesus was on earth, he taught people to follow God and make good decisions. When Jesus went back to heaven, God sent the Holy Spirit to live inside of us. The Holy Spirit teaches us to make good choices and reminds us to follow God's commandments.

If you're with a friend at school and that friend calls another student a bad name, does it make you feel uncomfortable? When you are about to break a rule,

like eating cookies without permission, do you feel uneasy? That is the Holy Spirit inside of you reminding you what is right and what is wrong. (Use recent examples to help children understand.)

There are other "voices" in our lives that try to drown out the voice of the Holy Spirit. What other voices can you think of that try to get us to make bad decisions? Peer pressure from friends to break rules. Commercials on TV that encourage us to be greedy—wanting more and more things. Anger in our minds that encourages us to say mean things or hit someone else.

B Activity

Choose one parent to represent the Holy Spirit. That parent stands on one side of the room. The children will start the activity from the opposite side of the room. **We will do this activity one child at a time. You will need to stay in another room where you can't see or hear what is happening until it is your turn.** (The Guiding Parent) **on the other side of the room represents the Holy Spirit. You will be blindfolded and must listen to** (The Guiding Parent's) **voice as he or she guides you across the room, around the tables, chairs, and couch until you reach him or her safely. The floor represents life and the tables, chairs, and couch represent obstacles/challenges in life. We are learning that if we listen to the voice of the Holy Spirit and follow his directions, then we can make it through life safely and avoid the obstacles.**

Do not tell the children that there will be other voices after they start walking blindfolded.

The guiding parent uses a quiet voice just loud enough for the child to hear. Do not raise your voice. The other parent or older children can position themselves to the right and left side of the path across the room. In louder voices, tempt the child to stop the activity or come to you for a snack instead of following the guiding parent. Say things like:

"Come over here. I've got a cookie for you."
"This activity is too hard! You don't want to go all the way through the house. Take off your blindfold."
"Turn this way. (The Guiding Parent) **is leading you the wrong way."**

Some kids will follow the voice of the guiding parent, and others might be tempted to follow the tempting voices from the side. After each child has a turn, discuss how easy or how hard it was to reach the goal. **Were you tempted? Was it hard to hear the quiet voice? What does this activity teach us about the Holy Spirit?**

Application

What are some things that you say to yourself when someone tries to tempt you? How do you prevent yourself from being caught up in the moment so that you don't end up doing the wrong thing?

Spend some time talking about how the Holy Spirit communicates with us to help us do the right thing and not fall into temptation.

Lesson 7:
HALLOWEEN: CHOOSE YOUR ATTITUDE

TEACHING GOAL: Attitude is not determined by circumstances. We choose our attitude.

1. Play theme song
2. Pray
3. Review last lesson
4. Lesson and discussion
5. Memorize: **I can choose to be; content with what I see.**
6. Close in prayer

SCRIPTURE: 2 Corinthians 11:23-27 "I have worked much harder, been in prison more frequently, been flogged more severely, and been exposed to death again and again. Five times I received from the Jews the forty lashes minus one. Three times I was beaten with rods, once I was stoned, three times I was shipwrecked, I spent a night and a day in the open sea, I have been constantly on the move.... I have labored and toiled and have often gone without sleep; I have known hunger and thirst and have often gone without food; I have been cold and naked."

Philippians 4:11-13 "...for I have learned to be content whatever the circumstances. I know what it is to be in need, and I know what it is to have plenty. I have learned the secret of being content in any and every situation, whether well fed or hungry, whether living in plenty or in want. I can do everything through him who gives me strength."

MATERIALS: Pumpkins
Colored markers or paint
Paper
Carving knife (optional)

IN ADVANCE: Photocopy the page with emotion faces, one copy for each child.

Words that are written in **bold** are when you, the parent, are speaking. Feel free to use your own words.

Big Idea:

Pointing to the seven faces, one at a time, ask the children what emotion the face represents. **How do you think a person with this face feels?** Write the emotions they suggest under each face. Present each child with one of the following situations or make up your own situations. **I'm going to tell you a short story and you tell me how the person in the story feels:**

- **There is a young girl who usually goes to bed at 8:00 pm. She stayed up late and it is now 4 hours past her regular bedtime. Which face reflects how she feels?**

- **A boy thought his mom was in the backyard and he was all alone in the house. He went into a dark closet to get a clean shirt, and he heard a voice say, "What are you doing?" Which face reflects how he feels?**

- **A girl just scored the winning goal in a soccer game. Which face reflects how she feels?**

- **A boy is trying to get the attention of his friends by pretending to fall down and telling funny jokes. Which face reflects how he feels?**

- **A girl just found out that her cat got outside and is missing. Which face reflects how she feels?**

The bottom face represents "content." **How do you think a person with this face feels?** Content is not laughing, not exactly the same as happy, nor is it sad. Content is a feeling of peace and satisfaction.

Give the children an opportunity to fill in the remaining faces with new feelings.

B Activity

In the same way, we can choose which attitude (or face) we wear, we're going to choose a face to put on a pumpkin. Hand out paper and markers. **Before we draw on our pumpkins with these markers (or cut out a face using knives), let's practice drawing the face on a piece of paper. You can choose to draw whatever face you want—a happy face, scary face, sad face, silly face, etc.** Draw the face and cut it out.

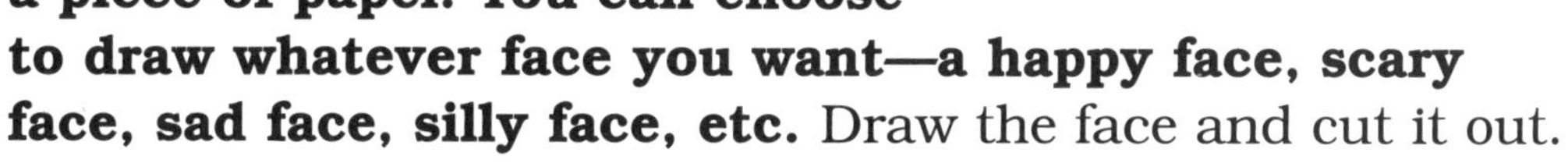

C Application

While carving the pumpkin tell the story of Paul. **One of the earliest Christians was a man named Paul. Paul wrote several of the books in the Bible. Paul was persecuted for being a Christian. Do you know what persecuted means?** People try to hurt you because of what you believe. **Paul also had very hard times as he traveled around to tell others about Jesus. Listen to all the things that happened to Paul.** Read 2 Corinthians 11:23-27.

Paul was put in jail just for telling others about Jesus. How do you think Paul felt in prison? Talk about what it must have been like to be in prison. Scared. Mad. Sad. **Paul tells us in one of his letters that he was "content" in prison. In fact, Paul tells us that he has learned to be content despite his circumstances.** Read Philippians 4:11-13. Point to the face that is content and explain again that content means feeling peaceful and satisfied. **Paul was content when he had food, and when he didn't have food. Paul was content when he was in jail, and when he was out of jail. How do you think you would feel if you were put in jail by mistake because someone mistook you for a thief?**

Paul teaches us that we can choose our attitude (what face we put on). We do not have to let circumstances, the things that happen to us, determine our attitude. Just as Paul chose to be content when he was in jail, we can choose to be content even during bad times. When we wake up in the morning, we can choose to be grumpy or we can choose to have good attitudes. When someone hurts our feelings, we can choose to let that ruin our day or we can choose to forgive and start over feeling happy.

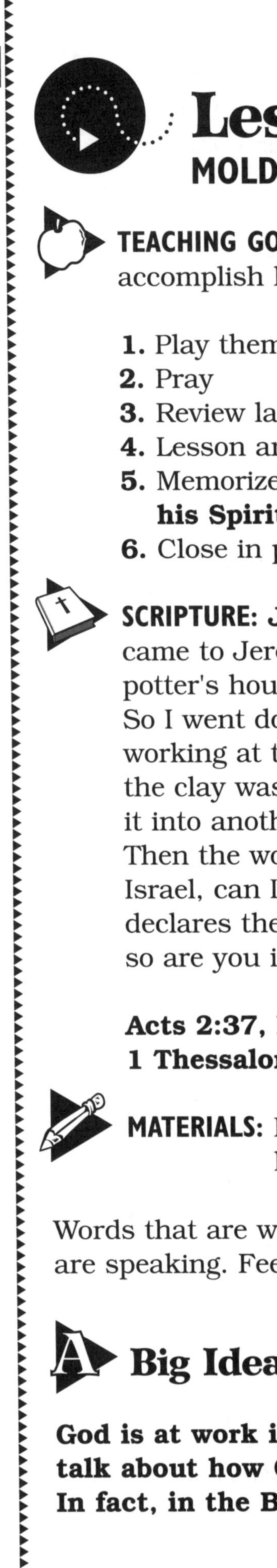

Lesson 8:
MOLD ME

TEACHING GOAL: God wants to mold our lives to accomplish his purpose.

1. Play theme song
2. Pray
3. Review last lesson
4. Lesson and discussion
5. Memorize: **In God and Jesus we abide; his Spirit is our inside guide.**
6. Close in prayer

SCRIPTURE: Jeremiah 18:1-6 "This is the word that came to Jeremiah from the LORD: 'Go down to the potter's house, and there I will give you my message.' So I went down to the potter's house, and I saw him working at the wheel. But the pot he was shaping from the clay was marred in his hands; so the potter formed it into another pot, shaping it as seemed best to him. Then the word of the LORD came to me: 'O house of Israel, can I not do with you as this potter does?' declares the LORD. 'Like clay in the hand of the potter, so are you in my hand.'"

Acts 2:37, Romans 12:2, Proverbs 4:14, and 1 Thessalonians 5:11

MATERIALS: Package of gum for each child (must be the kind with pieces individually wrapped in foil)

Words that are written in **bold** are when you, the parent, are speaking. Feel free to use your own words.

Big Idea

God is at work in our lives. So many scriptures talk about how God works and what he wants for us. In fact, in the Bible both God and Jesus used parables,

stories, and practical things around them to teach important lessons about God's work in our lives. Today we're going to learn some important things about God and his work in us by examining this pack of gum.

Activity

- **God wants us to open our hearts and let him in.** Read Acts 2:37. Pull the string that opens the top of the gum package to represent opening your heart.

- **As a Christian, God calls us to live for him. Therefore, we will need to change some things in our lives. We may need to change our surroundings or our actions. For example, we may need to change the television and movies that we used to watch or the language that we used to use before giving our life to Jesus. God also calls us to give up lying and stealing.** Read Romans 12:2. Remove the package around the sticks of gum to represent this change.

- **God may ask us to change some of our friends. We need friends who can help us live for Jesus.** Read Proverbs 4:14 and 1 Thessalonians 5:11. Some packages will have a piece of paper holding the sticks of gum together. Pull out one stick of gum to represent changing friends.

- **For our own good, God wants to mold us to his purposes. Even after we have changed our surroundings and developed friends who encourage us, we may still have something very specific that we need to change. Is there something with which you struggle that is displeasing to God? Pride? Attitude? Greed?** Take the cover off the individual piece of gum to represent the individual changes we need to make to align our lives with God's commandments.

- **Several places the Bible talks about God as a potter who molds us into a new person who will be used for his purposes. These changes are for our own good.**

These changes enable us to be used by God for great things. Read Jeremiah 18:1-6. Follow the directions included with this activity to mold a person out of the piece of foil.

INSTRUCTIONS FOR MOLDING A PERSON

1. Make a tear seven notches from the top and $^1/_3$ of the way toward the center of the foil gum wrapper. Make another tear on the other side. Roll the top section into a ball.

2. Repeat a second set of tears seven notches down from the first set of tears. Repeat a third set of tears seven notches down from the second set of tears. Make one more tear from the center bottom halfway up the remaining section of foil.

3. Mold the foil into a person by folding and twisting. The foil ball in the top section forms a head. Form arms below the head, then a middle section, and legs with the bottom section.

Application

No one is perfect. God is working in the lives of each of his children to grow us closer to himself. That means he uses different tools to mold us into his image. Over time we learn to sin less, think about others more, and follow God's commands.

What are some of the tools that God uses to grow us? Parents, teachers, experience, the Bible, friends, etc. **Think about some of the experiences you've had in the last month or so. What kinds of things is God teaching you?** Use this time to help children see how they are growing in maturity. Emphasize the reality that your child is in process and that's okay.

Lesson 9:
GOD'S PROTECTION

TEACHING GOAL: God is our protector.

1. Play theme song
2. Pray
3. Review last lesson
4. Lesson and discussion
5. Memorize: **As we live our lives each day; God and his angels protect our way.**
6. Close in prayer

SCRIPTURE: Psalm 91:11-12 "For he will command his angels concerning you to guard you in all your ways; they will lift you up in their hands, so that you will not strike your foot against a stone."

MATERIALS: Two sheets of red construction paper
One clear glass or plastic cup
One clear bowl or pitcher filled with water (it needs to be deep enough to completely submerge the cup without overflowing)

Words that are written in **bold** are when you, the parent, are speaking. Feel free to use your own words.

Big Idea

Understanding God's protection through his angels gives kids confidence instead of fear. Use this opportunity to help your kids develop a greater sense of God's protection.

Activity

Fill the bowl with water, set it in the middle of the table, and have the kids sit around the table. **The water in the bowl represents the world and its influences on us.** Take one of the sheets of red construction paper and crumple it into a ball. **This paper represents us.** Submerge the crumpled paper in the water and let it soak for a minute. **God places us in this world, just as we placed the paper in the water.** Pull the soaked paper out of the water. **How does the world affect us?** It hurts us, wrongly influences us, tempts us, etc.

In the Bible, we read that God is our protector. What are some ways that God protects us? After they've given some answers... **Why does God have angels?** Read Psalm 91:11-12. **The Bible says one way that God protects us is by sending his angels to watch over us.** Place the glass on the table. **The glass represents God's angels.** Take the second piece of red construction paper and crumple it up. **Again this paper represents us, and the Bible says God sends his angels to protect us.** Stick the paper into the bottom of the glass, representing us, covered by the protection of God's angels (make sure you secure the paper so that it will stay in the bottom of the glass).

Remember that God put us in this world. Invert the glass and submerge it to the bottom of the bowl. Hold it there for a minute, reviewing what happened to the paper that wasn't protected by the glass. Keeping it inverted, pull the glass out of the water and with your dry hand, remove the dry paper from the glass.

As we live our lives in this world, we can rely on God and his angels to protect us. That means that we don't have to live in fear. God protects us. It means that we don't have to worry about things. God protects us. It means that we don't have to get angry and get revenge on people. God protects us. It means that we can pray and talk to God when we feel upset. God protects us.

Lesson 10:
GOD-GIVEN DIFFERENCES

TEACHING GOAL: God makes each of us unique, that means in some ways, we are all different from each other. But we can be like Jesus by being friends with and helping people who are different from us.

1. Play theme song
2. Pray
3. Review last lesson
4. Lesson and discussion
5. Memorize: **Differences can be cool; when making friends at school.**
6. Close in prayer

SCRIPTURE: Matthew 8:1-3 "When he came down from the mountainside, large crowds followed him. A man with leprosy came and knelt before him and said, 'Lord, if you are willing, you can make me clean.' Jesus reached out his hand and touched the man. 'I am willing,' he said. 'Be clean!' Immediately he was cured of his leprosy."

Matthew 9:29-30 "Then he touched their eyes and said, 'According to your faith will it be done to you'; and their sight was restored."

Matthew 9:9-10 "As Jesus went on from there, he saw a man named Matthew sitting at the tax collector's booth. 'Follow me,' he told him, and Matthew got up and followed him. While Jesus was having dinner at Matthew's house, many tax collectors and 'sinners' came and ate with him and his disciples."

Matthew 15:21-22 "Leaving that place, Jesus withdrew to the region of Tyre and Sidon. A Canaanite woman from that vicinity came to him, crying out, "Lord, Son of David, have mercy on me!'"

Matthew 19:13-14 "Then little children were brought to Jesus for him to place his hands on them and pray for them. But the disciples rebuked those who brought them. Jesus said, 'Let the little children come to me, and do not hinder them, for the kingdom of heaven belongs to such as these.'"

MATERIALS: Name tags or paper and tape

Words that are written in **bold** are when you, the parent, are speaking. Feel free to use your own words.

Big Idea

Choosing the right friends is very important because friends influence us to do what's right or sometimes influence us to do what's wrong.

The type of differences we want to avoid are behavior differences that involve making bad choices. There are other differences between people that we do not want to avoid. These are differences that have to do with the color of a person's skin, how they talk, or physical differences.

In the book of Matthew we read how Jesus was friends with and helped people who were different:

ILLUSTRATION 1:

Jesus was kind to people who were sick (Mathew 8:1-3, 9:27-33). Leprosy—in Jesus' day, no one wanted to be around people with leprosy, but Jesus helped them. Blindness—blind people were treated poorly, but Jesus was kind to people who were blind.

IDEA: Some children have problems with their legs not working and they use wheelchairs. These kids may become your good friends.

You may know kids who wear thick glasses or braces. Other kids may make fun of them because they are different, but you can be like Jesus by being their friend.

ILLUSTRATION 2:

Jesus was kind to people who had different jobs (Matthew 9:9-10). Tax collectors—people did not like them, but Jesus was their friend.

IDEA: There will be kids in your school and neighborhood whose parents have all kinds of different jobs. We do not choose friends based on what kind of job their parents have, whether they are rich or poor, popular or unpopular.

ILLUSTRATION 3:

Jesus was kind to people from different cultures (Matthew 15:21-22). Canaanite woman—Jesus was a Jew, and in those days it was unpopular for Jews to be kind to people from Canaan. He helped a Canaanite woman with a sick daughter.

IDEA: You will meet kids who are from different cultures. They might be learning to speak English and be hard to understand. We need to be patient to listen and understand what they are saying, but we can be like Jesus and be friends with people from different countries and races.

ILLUSTRATION 4:

Jesus was kind to people of different ages (Matthew 19:13-14). Children—the disciples thought Jesus was too important to spend time with kids, but Jesus took time for children.

IDEA: You know people who are older and younger. Do not limit your friendships by only playing with the kids who are your age. When younger children are around, be patient and choose games that you can all play. Be respectful and polite to older children. Like Jesus, we can be friends with people of all ages.

B Activity

Everyone starts the game in the same room. One at a time, a child or adult leaves the room and changes three things about his or her appearance. A parent may want to help younger children with the changes. For example:

- Move a watch from one arm to the other
- Part your hair on the other side
- Take off one sock
- Put your t-shirt on backwards
- Untie a shoe
- Take off one earring
- Tuck in/untuck your shirt

When the person who has made the changes comes back into the room, the group has thirty seconds to discover the differences. Take turns being the "changer."

Differences can be fun. Looking different on the outside doesn't change who you are on the inside.

Make two kinds of name-tag size stickers, one kind with a round smiley face and the other kind with a square smiley face. Make the same number of each kind so everyone gets paired up. Have the group stand in a circle while the leader puts a sticker on each back.

Without using words, each person must find a partner who has a different sticker. They will need to find out what kind of sticker they have, and then they need to find someone with the other kind. (You may want to put a small piece of scotch tape on their lips as a reminder not to talk.)

Application

Differences can be fun. Sometimes, though, people are afraid of the differences that other people have. It takes a courageous person to look past differences and love someone for their heart. The next time you see someone who looks a little different, take some extra time to get to know him or her a little better. You'll be surprised at how you can learn some interesting things about other people even though they appear different on the outside.

Lesson 11:
ANGER

TEACHING GOAL: My anger leaves a mark on other people, and me too.

1. Play theme song
2. Pray
3. Review last lesson
4. Lesson and discussion
5. Memorize: **Anger hurts you; others, and me too.**
6. Close in prayer

SCRIPTURE: Psalm 37:7-8 "Be still before the LORD and wait patiently for him; do not fret when men succeed in their ways, when they carry out their wicked schemes. Refrain from anger and turn from wrath; do not fret—it leads only to evil."

Colossians 3:8, 12 "But now you must rid yourselves of all such things as these: anger, rage, malice, slander, and filthy language from your lips...clothe yourselves with compassion, kindness, humility, gentleness and patience."

MATERIALS: One or more bottles of carbonated soda (**CAUTION:** red may stain)
One or more bottles of a non-carbonated drink (like lemonade)
Newspaper
Marker
Masking or duct tape

Words that are written in **bold** are when you, the parent, are speaking. Feel free to use your own words.

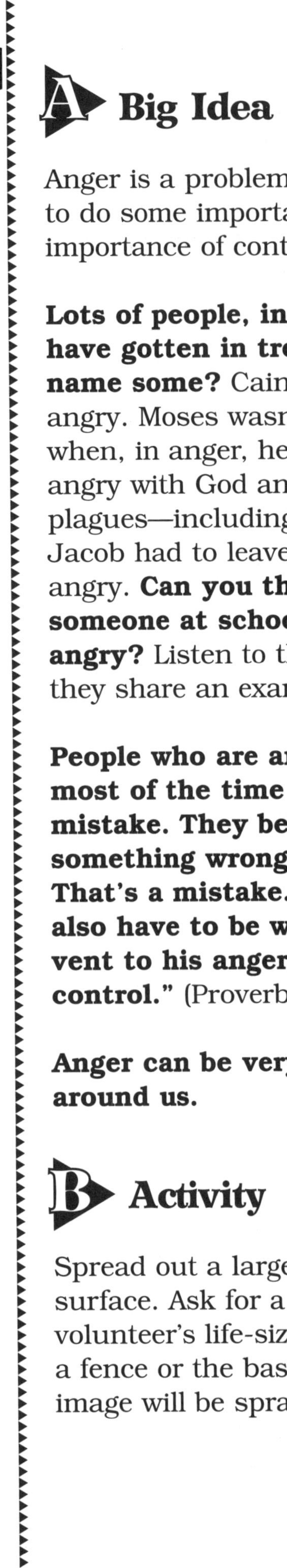

A Big Idea

Anger is a problem in many homes. You can use this lesson to do some important teaching about anger and the importance of controlling it.

Lots of people, including men and women in the Bible, have gotten in trouble because of their anger. Can you name some? Cain killed his brother Abel when he was angry. Moses wasn't allowed to go into the Promised Land when, in anger, he hit a rock with his staff. Pharaoh was angry with God and refused to obey him. This led to ten plagues—including one that caused the death of his son. Jacob had to leave home because his brother Esau was so angry. **Can you think of a time when you were angry or someone at school, in sports, or in the neighborhood was angry?** Listen to their answers. Avoid becoming defensive if they share an example from the family.

People who are angry usually believe they are right, and most of the time they are. But they are making a serious mistake. They believe that just because someone else did something wrong, then they have the right to get angry. That's a mistake. It's not good enough to be right. You also have to be wise. Proverbs says, "A fool gives full vent to his anger, but a wise man keeps himself under control." (Proverbs 29:11)

Anger can be very dangerous. Anger can hurt the people around us.

B Activity

Spread out a large amount of newspaper on or against a flat surface. Ask for a volunteer. Then, using a marker, trace the volunteer's life-size outline onto the paper. Tape the image on a fence or the base of a tree. (**NOTE:** The surface behind the image will be sprayed with soda.)

Carefully remove the tops from a bottle of carbonated soda and a bottle of non-carbonated drink. Drill or nail a small hole in the cap. Replace the cap before shaking. It is easier for younger children to cover the small hole with a thumb or finger. The small hole also causes the drink to spray farther. Ask for two volunteers, one to hold the carbonated and one to hold the non-carbonated drink. When directed, the volunteers will hold a thumb over the hole in the top of their bottle and shake the drink. Adults can do this part of the activity or younger children can use their palms to cover the bottle opening, which works great, but it's messier.

Read the story below, taking time to direct the drink shakers.

I'm going to tell you a story about two parents at a baseball game. The bottles of drinks represent the two parents. The image on the fence (tree) **represents a baseball umpire. When I direct you to do so, put your thumb over the top of your drink and start shaking.**

> **There were two parents at a very important baseball game. The winning team would go on to the state championship game. It had been a close game, and many times during the game the umpire had to make close calls that favored the other team.**

Okay, start shaking your bottle. When you feel the pressure building against your thumb, slide it off slightly and let the drink spray toward the umpire drawing. Take time for both kids to try and spray the image. The carbonated drink will spray and the non-carbonated drink won't spray. **The shaking represents going through a stressful or uncomfortable experience. The carbonation in the one soda represents anger. When life gets stressful, the person with anger inside will start to explode. They say and do things that hurt other people.**

> **Both parents were getting nervous. Their team was down by one run going into the last inning. With two outs, their best player came up to bat and hit a ball all the way to the fence. There was a runner on**

first, and if he could score it would tie the game. The runner made it around third base and started heading home. The outfielder picked up the ball and threw it toward home plate. It was going to be close! The runner slid, the catcher caught the ball and tagged the runner. Everyone watched as the umpire called the runner out!

Okay, keep shaking your bottle. When you feel the pressure building against your thumb, slide it off slightly and let the drink spray toward the umpire drawing. Take time for both kids to try and spray the image. **Remember, the bottles represent the parents. The shaking represents stress. The carbonation represents anger.**

The game was over and the parents' team lost. Both parents were disappointed but one exploded with anger! This parent started yelling bad words at the umpire. He went down to the fence and started screaming until his face turned red. His son, who was a player on the losing team, was very embarrassed by his dad's angry outbursts. Another person in the stands remembered seeing this angry man at church. The umpire was concerned that the angry parent might start a fight. The umpire called for security guards to help and they physically removed the parent from the ballpark.

The other parent, who was also disappointed, went down to the field and thanked the umpire for calling a good game. Both parents experienced the same stressful situation, but one was filled with anger and the other wasn't. They handled the same situation very differently.

Okay, shake your bottle some more. When you feel the pressure building against your thumb, slide it off slightly and let the drink spray toward the umpire drawing.

You might repeat the activity with other kids or adults who want to use the carbonated soda to play the part of the angry parent.

Application

In this story, who was hurt by the parent's anger? The umpire, the son, the parent himself, his church, others connected to the losing team, maybe even the winning team are all possible answers.

Invite volunteers (who don't have sticky hands) to read Psalm 37:7-8 and Colossians 3:8,12. **The Bible tells us to watch out for anger. Instead of anger, we need to show compassion. Instead of anger, we need to show kindness. Instead of anger, we need to show patience.**

One interesting thing about spraying soda is that it gets on you too. The same thing is true with anger. It not only makes a mess for others but it makes a mess of you. Angry people are unhappy people because they often don't know how to respond to correction well.

In the week ahead, look for real-life stories of anger from the newspaper or personal experience.

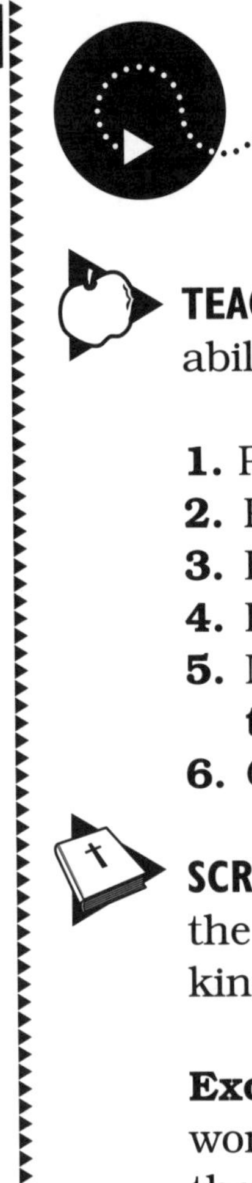

Lesson 12:
GOD USES OUR ABILITIES

TEACHING GOAL: God wants us to be aware of our abilities and use them for ministry.

1. Play theme song
2. Pray
3. Review last lesson
4. Lesson and discussion
5. Memorize: **God gives ability; so he can work through me.**
6. Close in prayer

SCRIPTURE: Exodus 31:3 "...and I have filled him with the Spirit of God, with skill, ability and knowledge in all kinds of crafts."

Exodus 31:1-11 List of names of skilled workers and work needing to be done for the tent of meeting (where the Israelites were going to worship).

MATERIALS: Paper
Pencil or marker
Peanut with shell
Legos, blocks, or other age-appropriate building materials

IN ADVANCE: Put the peanut in your pocket, out of sight.

Big Idea

A long time ago when Moses led the Israelites, they needed a place to worship. God knew that many people would be needed and that they would need special abilities and skills to complete what he wanted done. God provided the skills and knowledge to the people he had chosen to do his work. Some people think that only preachers or teachers are important to God's work.

That's not true. God needs people with all kinds of abilities and skills.

Activity

Let's build a building with these blocks. If we were to build a church, what kinds of materials would be necessary and what kinds of skills would be needed to complete the building? Help children to recognize all that goes into a building and how many skills are needed to make it. Architect, cement and brick layers, carpenters, plumbers, furnace and air conditioner installers, carpet layer, decorators, etc. While children are building, tell them about everything and everyone that was needed to build the Tent of Meeting.

MATERIALS	SKILLS
Gold, Silver, Bronze	Artistic Designers
Stones	Stone Cutters
Wood	Carpenters
Tent Material	Tent Makers
Ark	Craftsmen
Furniture	Furniture Makers
Special Clothing	Tailor
Perfumes and Incense	Scent Maker

A church is more than a building. The church includes people with different skills and talents. Who comes to mind when you think of someone who can preach? Pray? Teach Sunday School? Clean the building? Serve?

Be sure you have the peanut in your pocket. **I have something in my pocket that has never been seen or touched by anyone anywhere ever before. Would you like to guess what it is?** Play this up. Get the children to wondering how it got in your pocket if no one has seen or touched it before. After a few minutes of not being able to guess, pull out the peanut. Children will at first say they've seen a peanut before. Crack open the peanut. **You may have seen a peanut before, but this particular nut has never ever been seen or touched by human hands. It grew inside of this shell, and this is the very first time the shell has ever been opened.**

Like this ordinary peanut shell, we are ordinary people, but we have something inside of us that maybe no one has ever seen before. The peanut draws attention to something unique. Only God knows and has seen what grows inside this shell. This represents God-given gifts inside each one of us. God has given us skills and abilities that he wants to be able to use in our lives. He gives us knowledge and new skills every day. We might not be able to see it in ourselves or in other people but it's there, just like no one had ever seen the inside of this peanut.

Few skills can be learned overnight. It takes time and practice. God is building skills in you now that he will use later. We need to be ready when God wants to use our skills.

Application

Let's make a list of things you are learning to do and ways that God might use your abilities later.

EXAMPLES:

Learning numbers	Help with accounting at church Manage money better in order to give
Cooking	Help with meals for special events Cook for others, show hospitality

Parents, take this time to identify special gifts, talents, skills, and abilities you recognize in your children. Ask children to share special talents and skills they can use for God.

Lesson 13:
FAMILY MENTORS

TEACHING GOAL: Mentors are important for your child's spiritual development.

1. Pray
2. Lesson and discussion
3. Review last lesson
4. Lesson and discussion
5. Memorize: **Finding mentors who will pray; will help us do better every day.**
6. Close in prayer: Pray that God will show you additional mentors who can assist in the spiritual training of your children. Pray for wisdom and an opportunity to invite a family member or other mentor to take an active role in writing to your child.

SCRIPTURE: Deuteronomy 4:9 "Teach them to your children and to their children after them."

2 Timothy 1:5 "I have been reminded of your sincere faith, which first lived in your grandmother Lois and in your mother Eunice and, I am persuaded, now lives in you also."

Esther 2:7 "Mordecai had a cousin named Hadassah, whom he had brought up because she had neither father nor mother."

MATERIALS: Make or buy some cookies or other treat to give to the mentor.

Words that are written in **bold** are when you, the parent, are speaking. Feel free to use your own words.

A Big Idea

Mentors are important in the lives of our kids. Here's an example to consider.

The Ashtons are in their 70's. They do not have children, yet they have chosen to be proactive spiritual teachers in the life of their great-nephew, Tim.

Each month the Ashtons send Tim a $20 check with the recommendation that he use 10% to give to his church or some ministry. A second 10% is to be used to do something nice for a family member or friend. A third 10% is to be saved for his future—his education. The remaining 70% is Tim's to keep or use as he and his parents decide.

It's a "recommendation" because if Tim will write back and tell the Ashtons how he used the money they will send him another $20 the next month. If he does not write back with a full report—no check.

Along with the checks the Ashtons include stories of how God has been active in their lives and how the Christian faith is an important part of Tim's heritage.

Three years later, the Ashtons have a three-inch notebook filled with priceless letters to Tim and from Tim. Tim has given money to build a chapel at his school, to the church, to the homeless, and to missions that serve the poor.

The Ashtons have expanded their letters to include Bible quizzes and age-appropriate jokes.

Tim is blessed to have the Ashtons involved in his spiritual development. The Ashtons are blessed by building a growing relationship with Tim.

The goal of this lesson is for you, the parent, to invite a member of your extended family (or your spiritual mentor) to serve as a pen-pal mentor for your child. You can share the story of the Ashton's and you can share the notes from the activity section of this lesson.

The letter writing may or may not include sending money with stewardship training. It does need to be fun and include stories about the Christian faith. Put a time limit on the pen-pal relationship. Try one letter per month for a year. They can always choose to continue.

B Activity

The Bible includes stories of how God uses grandparents, cousins, brothers, and other adult relationships to support parents in spiritually training their children.

Read the book of Philemon with your children and write next to each verse characteristics of Paul that make him an effective mentor for his "son" Onesimus.

Verse 1 ______________________________

Verses 9 ______________________________

Verse 10 ______________________________

Verse 11 ______________________________

Verse 12 ______________________________

Verse 14 ______________________________

Verse15-16a ______________________________

Verse 16b ______________________________

Verse 18 ______________________________

Talk about the benefits of others in our lives. Talk about some of the significant people that help your family. Be sure to include grandparents, friends, teachers, church leaders, and other friends of your family.

Go and visit one of these people. Take (or mail) them a gift of cookies or another treat and spend a little time with them. Allow children to share some of their favorite Family Time Activities and then ask these friends to pray for your family.

 Application

We all need spiritual guidance. One of the ways God provides input for our lives is through other leaders and authorities. Spend time in the next week remembering some of the ways others have supported and encouraged your family.

Lesson 14:
ETERNITY

TEACHING GOAL: Eternity is a long time.

1. Play theme song
2. Pray
3. Review last lesson
4. Lesson and discussion
5. Memorize: **Eternal life, a gift to me; because in Jesus I believe.**
6. Close in prayer

SCRIPTURE: Romans 6:22 "But now that you have been set free from sin and have become slaves to God, the benefit you reap leads to holiness, and the result is eternal life."

Galatians 6:8 "The one who sows to please his sinful nature, from that nature will reap destruction; the one who sows to please the Spirit, from the Spirit will reap eternal life."

MATERIALS: Yardstick or ruler
Sidewalk chalk
Calculator

Words that are written in **bold** are when you, the parent, are speaking. Feel free to use your own words.

Big Idea

Sometimes we throw words around that we don't fully understand. Words like eternal, forever, and infinite are used to describe God, and we've become so accustomed to those words that we forget how immense God really is. There's a magical moment of worship that takes place when we try to understand an infinite idea with our finite minds. In this lesson you're trying to create that magical moment in the lives of your children. Be sure to turn that "wow" experience into worship of God. He truly is awesome, amazing, and wonderful.

Activity

The Bible tells us that Christians will live for eternity. How long is eternity? Forever. **You can't measure eternity but we're going to try.** Take the yardstick and have the children measure and mark the number of inches in a section of sidewalk. Mark at least 120 individual inches. Then mark ten inches at a time until you reach 1,000 inches. The goal is to make a large timeline on the sidewalk.

The very first mark is the beginning of your timeline. **Each inch represents a year of time.**

- **Let's mark off with a line the age of everyone in our family.** Using different color chalk, draw a line from the first mark to the mark that represents the current age of each family member.
- **Who is the oldest person we know?** Measure and mark with a line the age of the oldest person you know.
- **According to the Guinness Book of Records, the oldest living person is an American woman, Elizabeth Bolden, who was born on August 15, 1890 in Somerville, Tennessee.** (Effective as of 8/27/06) Measure and mark with a line the age of the oldest person currently alive.
- **Who is the oldest person in the Bible?** Let them guess. The oldest person whose age is given is Methuselah who lived to be 969. Measure and mark with a line the age of Methuselah.
- **If every inch represents a year, then how many years does our block represent?** Using steps or number of sections in the sidewalk, walk down the block and estimate the number of inches in your block.

You may need to use your calculator. Write the number of years on the sidewalk near your timeline. **Can you imagine living this long? Christians who live for eternity will live this long and even longer!**

- Pick a relative who lives in another state and estimate the distance to their home. For example: **Imagine if we were to measure from our home to Grammy's home 850 miles away. How many inches are in a foot?** 12. **How many feet are in a mile?** 5,280. **So, how many inches to Grammy's home?** 850 miles x 5,280 feet x 12 inches = 53,856,000 inches. Use the calculator and then write the number on the sidewalk next to the measurement of the block. **Can you imagine living for 53,856,000 years? Eternity is longer than that, in fact 53,000,000 is a small number compared to eternity.**

Application

The Bible tells us in the book of Romans (6:22) that eternity is a gift from God to those who believe in Jesus, the Son of God. "But now that you have been set free from sin and have become slaves to God, the benefit you reap leads to holiness, and the result is eternal life."

Lesson 15:
FORGIVEN SINS DISAPPEAR

TEACHING GOAL: Jesus died to forgive our sins. When our sins are forgiven, they are completely removed by God.

1. Play theme song
2. Pray
3. Review last lesson
4. Lesson and discussion
5. Memorize: **With Jesus' forgiveness our sins disappear; our guilt is gone and we have nothing to fear.**
6. Close in prayer

SCRIPTURE: Mark 14:12-16:19 Easter story

Psalm 103:12 "As far as the east is from the west, so far has he removed our transgressions from us."

Romans 5:8 "But God demonstrates his own love for us in this: While we were still sinners, Christ died for us."

Colossians 2:13-14 "When you were dead in your sins and in the uncircumcision of your sinful nature, God made you alive with Christ. He forgave us all our sins, having canceled the written code...he took it away, nailing it to the cross."

Romans 3:23 "For all have sinned and fall short of the glory of God."

Romans 6:23 "For the wages of sin is death, but the gift of God is eternal life in Christ Jesus our Lord."

MATERIALS: Flash paper
Pencil(s)
Sheet of Styrofoam or cardboard
Aluminum foil
Push pins
2 toothpicks
Matches
Safe knife

IN ADVANCE: Flash paper—special paper that burns "in a flash," leaving no ash. You can obtain flash paper from a local magic store.

Words that are written in **bold** are when you, the parent, are speaking. Feel free to use your own words.

Big Idea

In your own words, tell the Easter story (Mark 14:12-16:19), drawing attention to Jesus dying on the cross in order to be the final sacrifice for our sins. **What is a sin?** One way to define sin is: when we make what we want more important than what God wants. **The Bible tells us that everyone sins (Romans 3:23) and that a penalty must be paid for our sins (Romans 6:23). Why do you think Jesus had to die?** He died to pay the price for our sin so that we can live in heaven with a holy God. **Can you think of things that some people do that would be considered sin? What about not doing something that you know is right? For example, God wants us to show kindness in situations that are sometimes hard for us. If we choose not to be kind, are we sinning?** Yes.

Can you think of any sins that you've committed? (Parent, it may be beneficial for you to give an example of when you have sinned, asked for forgiveness, and it was given. Don't get into too many details or confess something upsetting to your child, but show that you are vulnerable and that God has helped you.) **How do you feel when you know you've sinned?** Guilty, stomach in knots, afraid of being caught, etc.

B Activity

Make the cross. Lay the sheet of Styrofoam or cardboard flat and carefully cut out a cross shape.

Cover the cross with aluminum foil to make it flameproof. Stick two toothpicks in a scrap piece of Styrofoam and impale the bottom of the cross on the toothpicks so that it is standing.

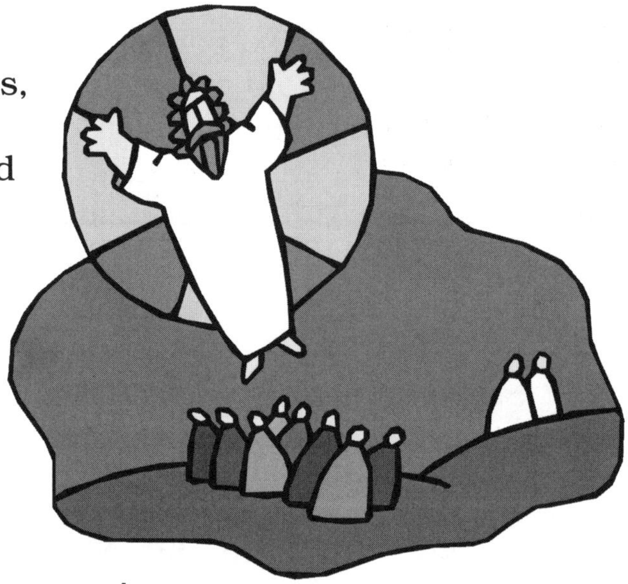

As you work on the cross, have children retell the story of Jesus' death and resurrection.

Give each person a piece of flash paper and pencil. **On this piece of paper, I want you to write a sin you've committed that needs to be forgiven. You do not have to show your paper to anyone else.** (Younger children may scribble a mark or draw something, as long as they know what it represents, or they may choose to have an adult write it for them.) Each person should write something.

Fold or crumple up your papers and pin them to the cross. **We are nailing our sins to the cross.** (Individually pin the pieces of paper in the middle of the cross and make sure the pieces touch each other.)

Jesus died for us and took our punishment. When we believe in him and ask for forgiveness, we can trust that we are forgiven. God loves us and wants us to be with him in heaven.

(Keep matches away from children and warn them that this is special paper that burns up quickly. Do not attempt this with regular paper. Step back after lighting.)

Light a match to the papers from the bottom. They will instantly go up in flames and then all trace of the papers will disappear without leaving any ashes.

Application

Where did the papers go? Shouldn't there at least be some ashes left? There is nothing left, just like Jesus taking away all our sins when he died on the cross. In Psalm 103:12 it says he [God] removes our sins as far as the east is from the west. When God forgives our sins they disappear completely.

Lesson 16:
DON'T SCHEDULE JESUS OUT

TEACHING GOAL: We need to make time for Jesus in our busy lives.

1. Play theme song
2. Pray
3. Review last lesson
4. Lesson and discussion
5. Memorize: **Being too busy will cause much strife; so keep the Lord Jesus in your everyday life.**
6. Close in prayer

SCRIPTURE: Luke 10:38-42 "As Jesus and his disciples were on their way, he came to a village where a woman named Martha opened her home to him. She had a sister called Mary, who sat at the Lord's feet listening to what he said. But Martha was distracted by all the preparations that had to be made...the Lord answered, 'you are worried and upset about many things, but only one thing is needed.'"

MATERIALS: Items to build an obstacle course:
Chairs, boxes, tires, benches, etc.
Rope
Timer
Balls (3 or 4 soccer and/or basketball and/or football)

Words that are written in **bold** are when you, the parent, are speaking. Feel free to use your own words.

Big Idea

Jesus went to the home of two women named Mary and Martha. Jesus sat down and started talking. Mary sat on the floor to listen to Jesus. Martha was busy fixing food and cleaning in the other room. Martha got upset because she was working hard and Mary was just sitting.

Jesus said that Mary was right to spend time with him and warned Martha not to get too busy with things that are not important.

Like Martha, our lives get busy and we do not take time to listen to Jesus. What keeps you busy? Going to school, playing soccer, taking swimming lessons, dance lessons, homework, T-ball, bike riding, choir.

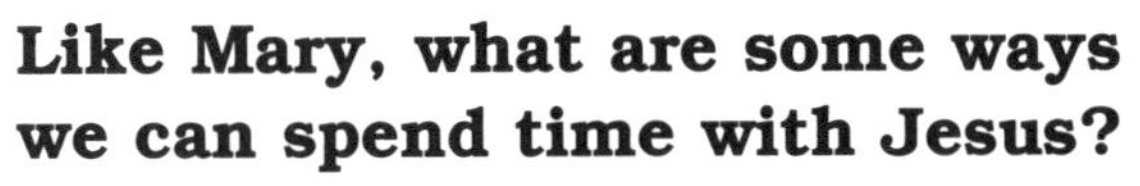

Like Mary, what are some ways we can spend time with Jesus? Prayer, reading or watching Bible stories, Family Times, lying quietly in bed and listening to hear Jesus. **We want to put Jesus first with our time. When we put Jesus first, there will still be plenty of time for other things.**

B Activity

Set up an obstacle course in a large room or outside. Use boxes, chairs, benches, tires, and other objects to make obstacles. With younger children, you may want to use a rope or heavy string to trace the route through the course. The string will show kids when to go over, under, or around obstacles.

The obstacle course represents living life. The obstacles on the course represent difficult times and changes that are beyond our control. Sickness. Moving. Accidents. **The balls represent things we choose to do with our time.** Sports. Entertainment. Playing with friends. Computer. **The finish line represents being with Jesus. The goal of this activity is to get to the end of the obstacle course so that we can be with Jesus.**

First we are going to run the course and time how fast we can go without carrying the balls. Time each child going through the obstacle course to see how long it takes.

Point out how quickly they can run through the course without carrying the balls. **You can get to Jesus and spend time with him quickly when you're not carrying the balls.**

Now we are going to run the course while carrying the balls. Remember the balls represent a busy life—all the things we choose to do with our time. Time each child running through the obstacle course trying to carry the balls. If you have enough time, let the kids run the course again. Point out what happens when the kids run the course with the balls and make the following applications:

It takes longer to complete the course. **When we get busy, we have less time to spend with Jesus. Too often we get to the end of a busy day and we've not taken any time to talk with Jesus or read our Bible. Busy people tend to be ruder, angrier, and less serving toward others. The obstacles represent things in life that keep us from being with Jesus. It is harder and takes longer to get through the course when there are obstacles. If we add too many activities to our lives, we won't spend enough time with Jesus.**

Kids drop the balls. **When we get busy, sometimes we "drop the ball." Too many sports and our grades may go down. We may end up doing an okay job at several tasks instead of doing a great job with fewer tasks.**

Kids let go of the balls to get past an obstacle. **When we are busy, it's harder to adjust to changes and difficult times. We may need to let go of some of the activities that keep us busy.**

Application

We need to keep our lives simple so that we can include spending time with Jesus. Martha was distracted by activities. Even though there is nothing wrong with any one activity, too many activities or any activity that keeps us from spending time with Jesus is a problem.

Lesson 17: ADDED VALUE

TEACHING GOAL: God loves us for who we are, not what we do.

1. Play theme song
2. Pray
3. Review last lesson
4. Lesson and discussion
5. Memorize: **Jesus adds value to me; that's what God will see.**
   or
   No matter what you've been through; God loves you.
6. Close in prayer

SCRIPTURE: Luke 15:11-32 Parable of the Lost Son

1 Peter 2:9 "But you are a chosen people, a royal priesthood, a holy nation, a people belonging to God, that you may declare the praises of him who called you out of darkness into his wonderful light."

MATERIALS: Paper
$20 bill
Baseball or other trading cards

Words that are written in **bold** are when you, the parent, are speaking. Feel free to use your own words.

Big Idea

Tell the story of the Prodigal Son in your own words. If your children are familiar with the story then you may ask your children to tell you the story. Fill in the gaps. Emphasize the unwise decisions that the younger son made and how he ended up eating with the pigs. He finally decided to come home and his dad met him with open arms, hugs, and kisses.

Even though the younger son made some bad choices and did some really bad things, his father still loved him. I want you to know that when you make bad choices and do bad things, it makes me sad but it does not change my love for you.

Jesus tells us this story because in some ways each one of us is the lost son, and he wants us to know that God our Heavenly Father loves us no matter what bad things we have done. God loves to hear us say, "I'm sorry," change our behavior, and come home.

Activity

Give each person a piece of paper. **Let's say that this is paper that we purchased to write on. Follow me and do what I do.** Go outside, in the garage or somewhere that you can get the paper really dirty. Rub it in the dirt. Flick a few drops of water on the paper and crumple it up. Crunch the paper into a small ball in your hand. Now, unfold it. **Is this still good paper for writing? Would your teacher accept homework turned in on this paper? Should we use it or throw it away?** Throw it away because it has lost its value as writing paper.

Take out the $20 bill. **Now, I'm going to do the same thing with this $20 bill.** Rub it in dirt, flick some water on it, crumple it up and then unfold it. **Should I throw it away?** NO! **Why not?** Because it is still worth $20. **We had two pieces of paper but one did not lose its value. The paper that is used to make a $20 bill is still valuable because the U.S. Government has added value to the piece of paper. The U.S. Government has said that even if it is dirty, wet, or crumpled, the bill is worth $20.**

Just like the U.S. Government has added value to the $20 bill, God has added value to you. When you become a Christian and ask Jesus to live in your heart, he makes you clean and new again. Jesus is the added value in our lives. So even if you make sinful choices, Jesus still lives

in you. When God looks at you he sees past all of the dirty sin to the beautiful heart Jesus is at work creating in you.

You can use baseball cards or other trading cards that are popular with the kids. If your kids are collectors you can ask them why certain cards have more value than others. This example uses baseball cards. In general, two things tend to add value to baseball cards: how rare the card is and how unique the player on the card is.

Here are two baseball cards. They are made out of the same kind of paper. Both have a picture on the front of a baseball player. If I tried to sell them, I would get a lot more for this one. Why? Let the children guess and share their answers. **This card has a picture of one of the best players in baseball. This card has a picture of a very average player. The card of the good player is worth more because he hits more home runs, steals bases, pitches better, etc. The picture of a better player adds value to the piece of cardboard and people are willing to pay more for it.**

You can compare a variety of cards and even share stories behind why you might have collected the cards. If they are cards that belong to your children, listen to them talk about the cards and learn why they value them.

Application

As Christians, believers in Jesus, we have added value. In the same way that the good player adds value to the card, Jesus adds value to us. Listen to what the Bible says about us, "You are a chosen people, a royal priesthood, a holy nation, a people belonging to God." We are royal priests. When God looks at us he sees Jesus in our lives. We have added value.

Lesson 18:
PRAYER CUBE

TEACHING GOAL: Prayer involves different components.

1. Play theme song
2. Pray
3. Review last lesson
4. Lesson and discussion
5. Memorize: **I will pray; every day.**
6. Close in prayer: Use the prayer cube.

SCRIPTURE: Matthew 6:9-13 "This, then, is how you should pray: Our Father in heaven, hallowed be your name, your kingdom come, your will be done on earth as it is in heaven. Give us today our daily bread. Forgive us our debts, as we also have forgiven our debtors. And lead us not into temptation, but deliver us from the evil one."

Ephesians 6:18 "And pray in the Spirit on all occasions with all kinds of prayers and requests. With this in mind, be alert and always keep on praying for all the saints."

MATERIALS: 1 copy of cube template (print in advance of the lesson)
Colored pencils and/or markers
Tape
OPTIONAL: Old magazines or computer clip art, scissors, and glue

IN ADVANCE: Photocopy the cube onto card stock, and cut it out so it's ready for the activity.

Words that are written in **bold** are when you, the parent, are speaking. Feel free to use your own words.

Big Idea

Prayer is an important part of our communion with God. There are lots of ways to pray and this lesson will expand a child's understanding of prayer. Typically we have mealtime prayers and bedtime prayers and we usually follow a certain format. Some families just use memorized prayers to offer at these times.

Learning how to pray spontaneously is an important part of everyone's spiritual growth. Practice this fun activity with your kids and talk about the different ways we can pray and talk to God as our Father.

Activity

We are going to create a "Prayer Cube" that we can use when we pray. Just toss the cube and pray for whatever is on top. Hold up the prayer cube diagram. **But first, let's read a couple of verses that talk about prayer. These verses will give us prayer ideas that we can put on each side of our prayer cube.**

In Matthew 6:9 Jesus teaches us how to pray. Invite a volunteer to read Matthew 6:9-13. **This is called "The Lord's Prayer." Let's look at each part of this prayer. It will give us five ideas for five sides of our prayer cube.**

Read: **"Our Father in heaven, hallowed be your name." On the first side of our cube we are going to put PRAISE GOD. God is holy, all-powerful, all-knowing, all-loving, and our prayers need to include thanking and praising God.**

Read: **"Your kingdom come, your will be done on earth as it is in heaven." On the second side of our cube we are going to put GOD'S WILL. God tells us in the Bible and through his Spirit that lives inside of us what to do, what to say, and how to think. We need to pray for God's help in making good choices, having a positive attitude, and keeping our thoughts pure.**

Read: **"Give us today our daily bread." Everything we have is a gift from God. In our prayers we can thank God for our home, food, clothes, job, school, and safety. DAILY NEEDS will go on the third side of our cube.**

Read: **"Forgive us our debts, as we also have forgiven our debtors." FORGIVENESS can go on the fourth side of our cube. When we pray, we need to ask God to forgive us for times when we made wrong choices. When we sin—lying, stealing, hurting others, disobedience, mean spirit, when we deliberately do things we know are wrong.**

Read: **"And lead us not into temptation, but deliver us from the evil one." We need WISDOM to help us make right choices. We can pray for God to help us see when we are being tempted to do something wrong and then to turn away from doing what is wrong. It is also wise to pray for God's protection against Satan, the evil one. We will put WISDOM on the fifth side.**

There are six sides and we only have five topics. Invite a volunteer to read Ephesians 6:18. **The Apostle Paul, who wrote Ephesians, tells us that we can pray for anything! So on the sixth side we will put ANYTHING. At prayer time, when we roll the cube, if this side is on top then you can choose to pray about anything that is important to you.**

Let's make and decorate the prayer cube. Write one of the six key phrases on each side of the prayer cube: PRAISE GOD, GOD'S WILL, DAILY NEEDS, FORGIVENESS, WISDOM, ANYTHING. You could type these on a computer and invite family members to choose different fonts for each word.

Next, on each side of the cube draw words, pictures, or images that represent the key words. You may want to assign decorating one or two sides to each family member. You could decorate with pictures from old magazines or clip art and pictures from the computer.

At mealtime or any other time that you pray, take turns rolling the cube and praying for what shows up on top.

C Application

Helping children feel comfortable with prayer is an important part of their spiritual development. Take time and use creative ways to pray in order to expand their comfort level. If children don't want to pray, you may decide to have them watch you.

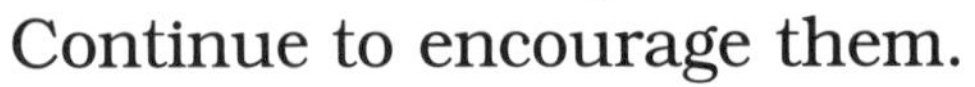

Continue to encourage them. With practice your children will learn how they can offer prayers to God at any time.

Here are some other creative ways to encourage prayer:

- Use one-word prayers. Everyone thinks of one word based on the theme (things we're grateful for, people that need prayer, etc.).
- Pray with your eyes open.
- Sing a prayer to God.

Close the lesson by giving each person a turn rolling the cube and praying for what shows up on top.

CUBE

Lesson 19:
GOD'S DIRECTION FOR OUR LIVES

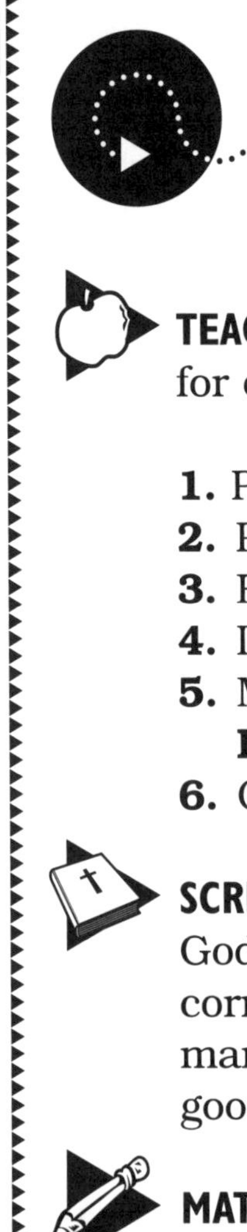

TEACHING GOAL: The Bible teaches God's direction for our lives.

1. Play theme song
2. Pray
3. Review last lesson
4. Lesson and discussion
5. Memorize: **Our way leads astray; so on God's path I'll stay.**
6. Close in prayer

SCRIPTURE: 2 Timothy 3:16-17 "All Scripture is God-breathed and is useful for teaching, rebuking, correcting and training in righteousness, so that the man of God may be thoroughly equipped for every good work."

MATERIALS: Car and prepared directions

IN ADVANCE: Prepare directions leading to a special surprise (ice cream, dinner, park, play area, etc). If your child can't read, you might use symbols of a right hand and left hand for making turns, and draw stop signs and traffic lights. You also may want to include landmarks like the bank, video store, and grocery store.

Words that are written in **bold** are when you, the parent, are speaking. Feel free to use your own words.

Big Idea

Sit in a circle with the Bible in the middle. Talk about how God teaches us through the Bible what is right and what is wrong. When we talk about God being in our heart and God walking with us, part of that refers to us reading the Bible and learning what the Bible says. The Bible contains "God's direction for our lives."

- **We go to church because God tells us to get together with other Christians.**
- **We pray because God tells us to talk with him though prayer.**
- **We give to missions because God tells us to give to those in need.**
- **God warns us not to lie because it leads to trouble.**
- **God teaches us to obey our parents.**

B Activity

Give one of the kids the directions. Tell your family that the directions will lead to a nice surprise. Load up in the car with a parent driving and a child reading the directions. As the parent drives, he or she ignores the directions the child is giving, saying **"I know what I'm doing. I'll get there my own way."** (Be prepared that the child may get upset, so try to keep the trip light and focused on learning a lesson.)

The driver eventually ends up at a dumpster (or dead end, etc.). He or she finally admits, **"I'm lost,"** and apologizes for not following the directions. Also emphasize that when we go our own way and ignore God's directions, we end up "in the dumps" or in a yucky situation.

Go back home and start over, but this time follow the directions, ending up at your surprise destination.

Application

You may want to incorporate this application section while you drive to the fun destination, or pause in the car for a few minutes after you arrive.

The Bible is our set of directions and it gives us instructions about how to live. Some people don't obey the Bible and they get lost. When we follow God's Word we have peace and joy in our lives. When we don't follow his direction, then we end up in the dumps. It's very important to follow the directions God has given us for life. We find those directions in the Bible.

Lesson 20:
HITTING THE TARGET

TEACHING GOAL: As Christians, our target is to live a holy life. God gives us the Bible, the Holy Spirit, and the example of Jesus' life to help us live a holy life.

1. Play theme song
2. Pray
3. Review last lesson
4. Lesson and discussion
5. Memorize: **God gave me Jesus, the Bible, and the Holy Spirit; so I can hit the target instead of landing near it.**
6. Close in prayer

SCRIPTURE: Psalm 119:9-11 "How can a young man keep his way pure? By living according to your word. I seek you with all my heart; do not let me stray from your commands. I have hidden your word in my heart that I might not sin against you."

Romans 8:26-27 "The Spirit helps us in our weakness. We do not know what we ought to pray for, but the Spirit himself intercedes for us with groans that words cannot express. And he who searches our hearts knows the mind of the Spirit, because the Spirit intercedes for the saints in accordance with God's will."

1 Peter 2:21-22 "To this you were called, because Christ suffered for you, leaving you an example, that you should follow in his steps. 'He committed no sin, and no deceit was found in his mouth.'"

MATERIALS: One 15-foot length of fishing line or dental floss per child
One large balloon per child
One straw per child
Tape
A bull's-eye target (provided)
Construction paper (may use colored paper or color onto white paper)

IN ADVANCE: Photocopy onto construction paper the bull's-eye target at the end of this lesson. Put a small hole in the center of the target. Pass one end of the fishing line through the small hole and tape the end of the line to a wall at the children's eye-level. Tape the target to the wall so that the middle hole is centered over the taped fishing line. The unattached end of the fishing line will hang down until you need it later.

This lesson is best done with another family or two. In advance tell others about your Family Time experience and invite them to join in with you for an evening. Not only will your friends enjoy having Family Time, but they may catch a vision for having their own regular Family Times too.

Words that are written in **bold** are when you, the parent, are speaking. Feel free to use your own words.

Big Idea

There's a right way to live and a lot of wrong ways to live. Finding that right way requires that we read the Bible and that we allow God to work inside of us to help us. God wants each of us to live a holy life. That means that we are making right choices. He also gives us the strength inside to do the right things when they are difficult.

In our lesson today we learn that we can't live a holy life on our own. We need the tools that God has given us to accomplish this and be successful.

Activity

Hitting the Target. **God wants us to live a holy life, right? The target represents living a holy life. The balloon represents us. Let's see if we can throw the deflated balloon and hit the target from 15 feet away.** Give each child a turn, but most likely the balloon will miss the target. **Like trying to throw a deflated balloon, we can't hit the target of a holy life on our own.**

Pick up the loose end of the fishing line. **God knew we couldn't live a holy life on our own, so he gave us the Bible as a guide. This string represents the Bible. It points the way to a holy life.** Now that the kids can see the path to a holy life, give them another chance to throw the balloon at the target.

God also sent his son Jesus as an example for us on how to live a holy life. The straw represents Jesus. Feed the line through the straw, pull the line tightly but be careful not to pull the other end off the wall. Push the straw down the fishing line to the target. **Jesus was the only one who could live a holy life on his own. He serves as our example.**

Have the kids try one more time to throw the balloon to the target now that they have the guide of the Bible and the example of Jesus. **God knew we would need one more thing to help us live a holy life. When we become a Christian, God gives us his Holy Spirit to encourage, strengthen, and teach us.** Hold up a balloon. **Remember that the balloon represents us, so the air inside the balloon represents the Holy Spirit in our lives.**

Blow up a balloon, pinch shut but don't tie the opening. Tape the side of the inflated balloon to the bottom of the straw (remember the straw is on the fishing line). **To live a holy life we need to imitate the example of Jesus (the straw), rely on the power of the Holy Spirit (the air in the balloon), and follow God's instructions in the Bible (the string).** Keep a little slack in the line and hold your end slightly higher than the end attached to the wall. Let go of the balloon, allowing the escaping air to push the balloon to the target.

ADDITIONAL FUN: Balloon races. After the end of this activity, you may set up multiple lines with straws and allow the children to have balloon races.

Application

What do we learn from this lesson? What does the target represent? A holy life. **What tools do we need to get the balloon to the target every time?** We need the string, the straw, and the air in the balloon. **What do these represent?** The Bible, Jesus, and the Holy Spirit.

Holiness has to do with the choices that we make every day. We choose how we're going to talk to each other with honor, how we share generously with others, and even when we correct others, that we do it graciously. Let's think this week about living the holy life that God offers to us.

BULL'S-EYE TARGET

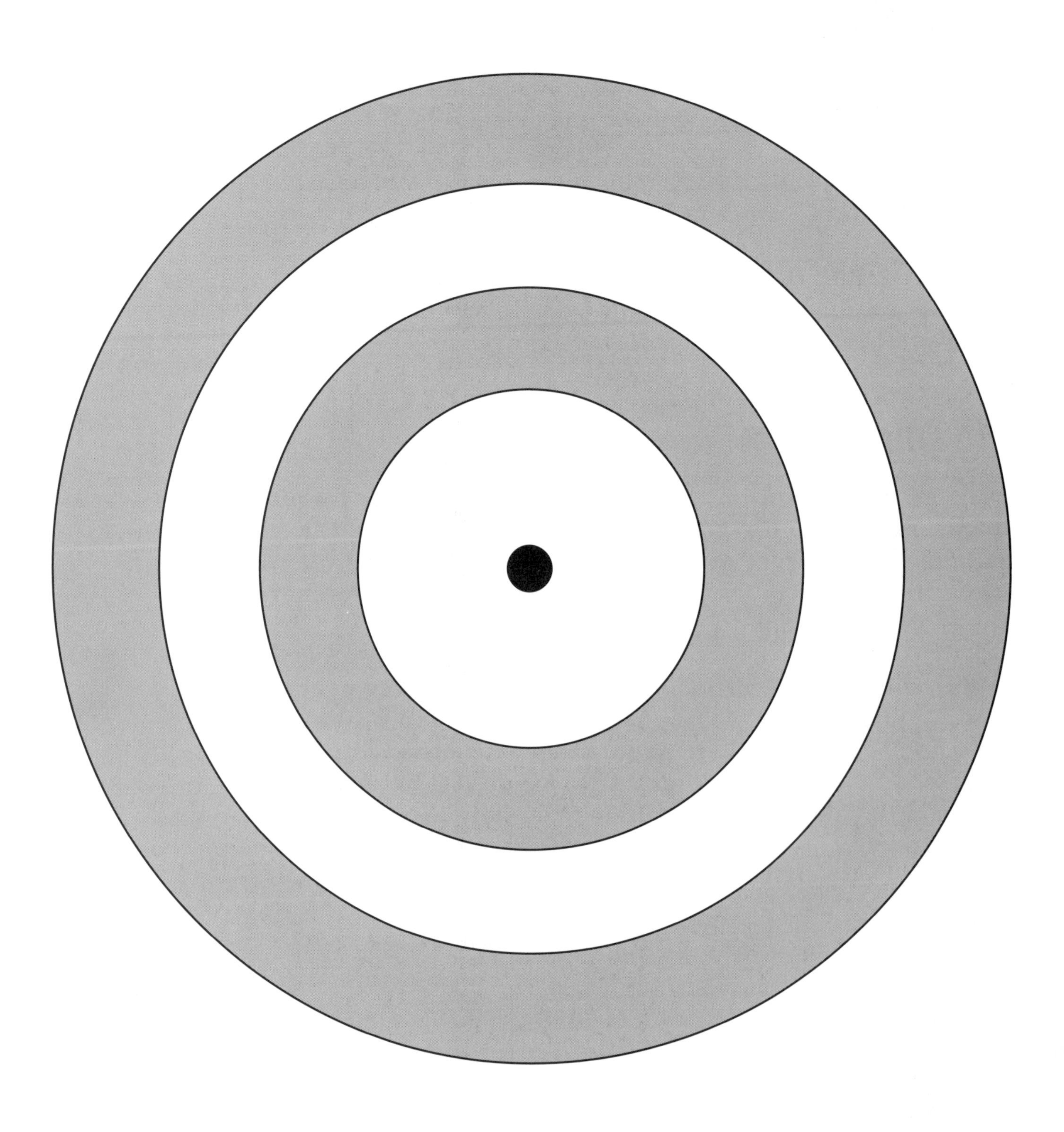

Index

Seeing is Believing (ALL AGES)

Playing for Keeps (ALL AGES)

Running the Race (ALL AGES)

Wiggles, Giggles, & Popcorn (PRESCHOOLERS)

Index

Bubbles, Balloons, & Chocolate (PRESCHOOLERS)

Tried and True (TEENS)

To view lists alphabetized by title, topic, and scripture visit www.famtime.com

You Will Benefit from **OTHER RESOURCES** for **YOUR FAMILY**

Discover practical, biblical tools to help you build strong bonds in your relationships at home. Find parenting books, CDs, and DVDs to help you parent from a heart-based perspective. Children's curriculum is available to teach your child the same concepts you are learning. **Free Email Parenting Tips** encourage you on a weekly basis. **Learn more at www.biblicalparenting.org.**

Receive practical, biblical parenting advice a couple times a week in your inbox. Sign up online at www.biblicalparenting.org. Also available in Spanish. Visit www.padresefectivos.org.

Sign up for Free Email Parenting Tips now. (You can remove yourself from the list at any time.) Your email address will not be shared or sold to others.

To learn more give us a call or visit biblicalparenting.org

76 Hopatcong Drive
Lawrenceville, NJ 08648-4136
Phone: (800) 771-8334
Email: parent@biblicalparenting.org